交通与土地利用的创新
——寻找交通堵塞的解决之道

[美]里德·尤因 著
李 翅 译

中国建筑工业出版社

著作权合同登记图字：01-2006-3822号

图书在版编目（CIP）数据

交通与土地利用的创新——寻找交通堵塞的解决之道／（美）尤因著；李翅译．
北京：中国建筑工业出版社，2013.10
ISBN 978-7-112-15690-0

Ⅰ.①交… Ⅱ.①尤… ②李… Ⅲ.①交通堵塞－交通规划－研究 Ⅳ.①U491

中国版本图书馆CIP数据核字（2013）第183708号

Transportation & Land Use Innovation：When You Can't Pave Your Way Out of Congestion
Copyright©1997 American Planning Associates.
Translation©2014 China Architecture and Building Press
All rights reserved.

本书由美国规划协会授权翻译出版

责任编辑：程素荣 张鹏伟　　责任设计：董建平　　责任校对：肖　剑　赵　颖

交通与土地利用的创新
　　——寻找交通堵塞的解决之道
[美]里德·尤因　著
李　翅　译
*
中国建筑工业出版社出版、发行（北京西郊百万庄）
各地新华书店、建筑书店经销
北 京 嘉 泰 利 德 公 司 制 版
北京云浩印刷有限责任公司印刷
*
开本：880×1230毫米　横1/16　印张：7　字数：150千字
2014年2月第一版　　2014年2月第一次印刷
定价：25.00元
ISBN 978-7-112-15690-0
　　　（24506）

版权所有　翻印必究
如有印装质量问题，可寄本社退换
（邮政编码　100037）

目 录

第一章　导言 ... 1
　　　　道路权利与使用者权利

第二章　机动性的新方法 ... 5
　　　　在州级层面的行动
　　　　联邦政府也要有所行动

第三章　机动性规划要素 ... 9
　　　　1　远景规划
　　　　2　土地利用规划
　　　　3　路网设计
　　　　4　城市设计
　　　　5　交通工具

第四章　基于可达性的土地规划 ... 19
　　　　从不同角度来看可达性
　　　　区域
　　　　社区
　　　　活动中心

第五章　交通需求管理 ... 27
　　　　没有什么新奇的或者再看看？
　　　　雇主的重要作用
　　　　停车场的重要作用
　　　　其他拼车奖励措施
　　　　比公共出行更加实惠的方法
　　　　为非工作群体的TDM

第六章	交通系统管理	35
	道路权利的再分配	
	可达性管理	
	道路交叉口的控制	
	先进的交通管理系统	

第七章	增强运输服务	43
	交通运输走廊和节点	
	扩展服务领域	
	减少交通运行时间	
	非传统服务	
	操作经济体	

第八章	有利于行人和骑自行车人的设计	59
	良好的意愿	
	让旅途简短	
	让旅行安全	
	使旅行有趣	
	交通减速	

第九章	不只是速度——新一代交通水平评价指标和方法	71
	交通范例转变	
	州和联邦法律的变化	
	来自国家政府的导则	
	统一的指标评价方法	
	结束语	

注释 83

致 谢

作者希望特别感谢来自于佛罗里达社区事务部门的本·斯塔雷特（Ben Starrett）的帮助，他提供了这本书的最初想法，引导其发展，并使其顺利发展。最初的许多插图由两个在南佛罗里达大学的佛罗里达社区设计和研究中心聪明的研究员迈克尔·福尔哈伯（Michael Faulhaber）和克里斯托弗·乔伊纳（Christopher Joiner）完成。

当时在佛罗里达大西洋大学（Florida Atlantic University）/佛罗里达国际大学（Florida International University）联合中心，现在在科勒尔斯普林斯供职的克里斯汀·赫夫林（Christine Heflin）提供了调查研究和编辑的援助。版式设计由布劳沃德社区学院的苏珊娜·兰伯特（Suzanne Lambert）、佛罗里达大西洋大学/佛罗里达国际大学联合中心的玛丽贝丝·迪安娜（MaryBeth DeAnna），以及佛罗里达国际大学的查克·库先（Chuck Kooshian）完成。以下各个领域的顶级专业评论家提供了如下很有帮助的评论和建议：

Visioning
Rick Bernhardt
Department of Planning and Development, City of Orlando
Ken Hirsch
Hirsch Architects, Inc., Boca Raton

Land Planning and Urban Design
James Moore
University of South Florida, Tampa
Chris Sinclair
TransCore, Orlando

Street Network Design
Walt Kulash
Glatting Jackson Inc., Orlando

Travel Demand Management
Bill Mustard
Florida State University, Tallahassee
Phil Winters and Dan Rudge
University of South Florida, Tampa

Transportation System Management/Access Management/
Intelligent Transportation Systems
Ken Courage
University of Florida, Gainesville

Mike Pietrzyk
University of South Florida, Tampa
Gary Sokolow
Florida Department of Transportation, Tallahassee

Enhanced Transit Service
Dan Boyle and Ron Sheck
University of South Florida, Tampa
Jim Charlier
Charlier Associates, Inc., Orlando
Gregg Thompson
Florida State University, Tallahassee

Bicycle and Pedestrian Facilities
Dan Burden and Pat Greason
Florida Department of Transportation, Tallahassee
Martin Guttenplan
Florida State University, Tallahassee

Measuring Mobility
Rick Hall
Hall Planning & Engineering, Tallahassee
Doug McLeod
Florida Department of Transportation, Tallahassee
Clark Turner
Department of Planning, City of Miami

第一章 导言

许多城市的交通堵塞已经达到饱和，如今的机动交通比20世纪的马车还要慢。

佛罗里达州塔拉哈西市道路特别委员会[1]

这段话写于1954年。尽管数十亿美元用于道路改造工程，但交通堵塞的情况似乎变得更加严重。据估计，佛罗里达州的居民每天因交通堵塞总共消耗掉大约300万小时的时间[2]。

我们必须找到办法以满足人们所希望的更低成本的交通需求，或者可以做得更好，去减少人们这么多的机动交通需求。这本手册提供了切实可行的建议，以减少交通堵塞、对机动车的依赖和车辆行驶里程。尽管是为非相关专业人员编写，但为满足专业人员更深入的研究，本手册提供了详尽的尾注。

道路权利与使用者权利

车辆行驶里程（VMT）的上升速度惊人。在1983—1990年之间，美国的车辆行驶里程增加了42%，约为人口增长速度的7倍[3]。我们的道路建设速度跟不上车辆行驶里程的增长速度。由于道路承载力的提高使得高峰时间的交通更加严峻，高峰时间交通法一直在缓解这一情况的恶

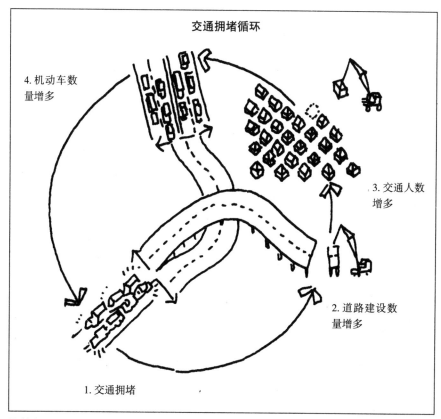

资料来源：引自绿带联盟，振兴可持续发展的都市，进入21世纪的海湾地区保护和发展指引，旧金山，加利福尼亚州，1989年。

化[4]。根据现有的乐观估计，公路里程1%的增长，在仅仅四年后，便会导致大城市地区的车辆行驶里程增加0.9%[5]。

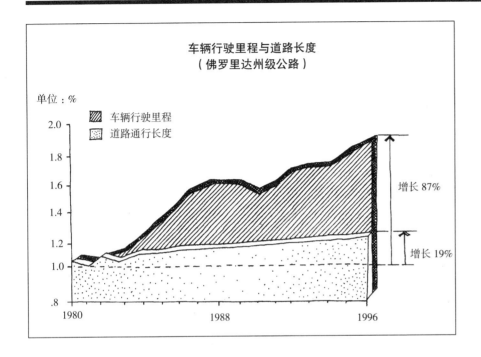

即使我们拥有资源,但我们真的要提供所需的全部道路承载力吗?机动车的平均使用成本很低,约为每英里 11 美分;折旧、保险和其他固定成本加起来约合每英里 29 美分[6]。这一成本依然很低,机动车使用者可以自行承担。

但是,当你从一个普通纳税人的角度来看道路补贴时,这些补贴包括了近乎免费的停车成本,以及各种各样的社会成本,如空气污染和无补偿的交通事故损失,机动车的使用成本是相当昂贵的[7]。若将所有的社会成本转嫁于机动车使用者,则每加仑燃油税需上调1.8～3美元(具体数值取决于你相信谁的预测)[8]。

此外,交通距离远和交通速度快并不是机动性的全部。37%的佛罗里达州居民成为了这样或那样的交通弱势群体,如残疾人、无法驾驶的小孩和老人,以及没钱买车的穷人[9]。在以汽车为中心的社会,这些群体正经历着被社会学家称之为可达性剥夺的问题[10]。这些负面影响都有据可查[11]。

因此,在本手册中,对于通行能力的理解与通常的定义有所不同。这里不是指我们利用机动车交通出行又远又快的能力,而是无论年龄和地位,人们以对于他们自己和社会来说,用相对适中的成本从事他们所希望的活动的能力。

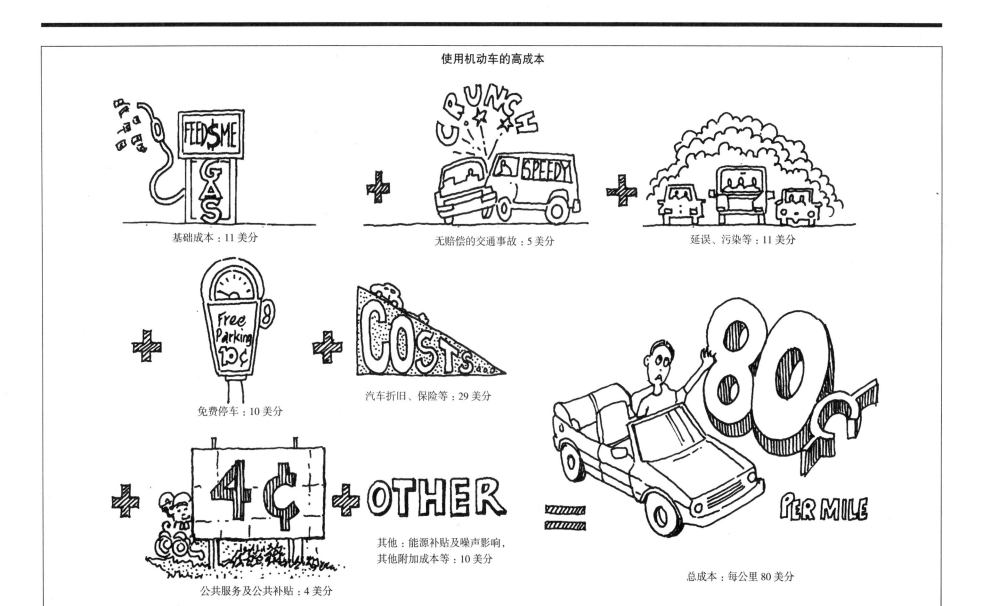

第二章 机动性的新方法

交通的供给因为经济、社会和环境等因素正受到越来越多的阻碍……庆幸的是,"减少"人们对于交通基础设施的需求而不降低个人的交通流动性已成为可能。

城市发展模式研究市长专责小组[12]

佛罗里达州1985年的城市发展管理法是开创性的。新泽西州、缅因州、佛蒙特州、罗得岛州、佐治亚州、华盛顿州和马里兰州都借鉴了佛罗里达州这一法律概念,甚至直接借鉴其法律条文。

然而,经过几年的实践,佛罗里达州的增长管理并未取得预期成果是个不争的事实。人们希望道路的运行能力在既定的服务水平之上,这导致了发展向城市外围地区转移,而这一地区本来就存在着交通供给过剩的问题。相比于其他方法,道路建设备受青睐,主要是因为道路的建设至少会暂时减少交通堵塞。城市的蔓延有增无减,而实际上,这更加剧了人们对机动车的依赖。

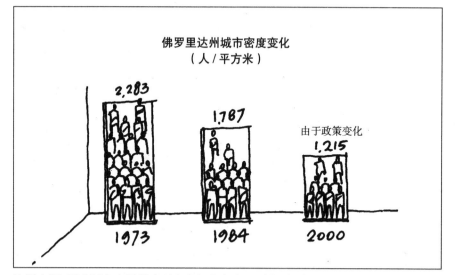

资料来源:引自城市发展模式研究市长专责小组,最终报告,佛罗里达州社会事务部,塔拉哈西市,佛罗里达州,1989年。

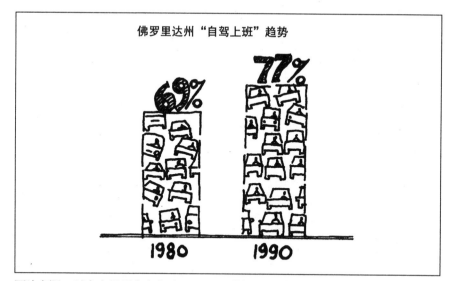

图片来源:城市交通研究中心(CUTR),佛罗里达州通勤人口研究,南佛罗里达大学,坦帕,1994年。

在州级层面的行动

鉴于此，1992年，社会事务部和佛罗里达州交通运输部采取了相应的举措，包括给予城市和县更多的自主权，放宽城市中心区及城市其他活动中心的道路服务水平标准（即交通并管理区域，简称TCMAs）。反过来，城市和县要积极推广替代单人驾驶自用车的交通方式。

1993年，佛罗里达州立法机构将TCMAs纳入该州永久性法律的一部分，并针对城市密集区及城市更新地区，制定了与一般道路服务等级标准不同的特殊区域（即交通特殊区域，简称TCEAs）[13]。新的法律和实施细则规定城市化地区要以丰富多样的交通方式，配合交通需求管理计划、交通运输系统管理措施以及行人和自行车交通设施改善，来取代落后的交通、运输和综合规划中港口交通等方面内容[14]。

联邦政府也要有所行动

佛罗里达州对机动性的新认识呼应了联邦政府的政策变化。根据美国《洁净空气法1990年修正案》，空气受到污染的大城市地区必须遏制汽车尾气排放的增长或者有效降低汽车尾气的排放水平（具体措施取决于空气污染的严重性）。对于还没有达到国家空气质量标准的地区和最近刚刚达标且需要保持的地区（包括佛罗里达州三个空气质量"保持区"），交通运输规划、计划、项目必须符合空气质量规划[15]。修建公路不再是唯一的解决方式。交通治理措施必须到位以使相应地

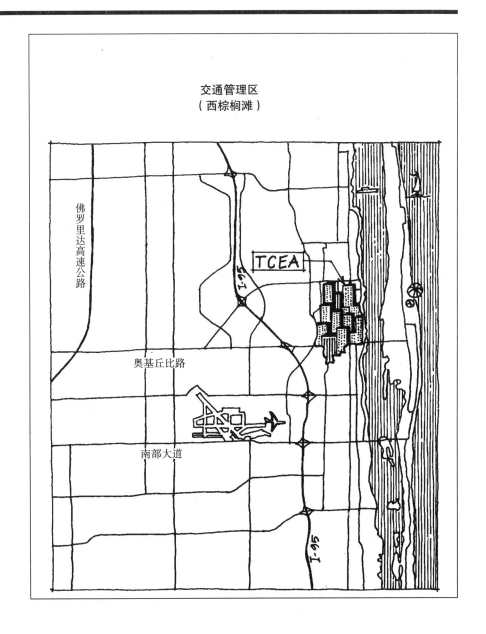

交通管理区
（西棕榈滩）

区符合国家标准要求。联邦政府的措施包括了许多与早前佛罗里达州1993年的城市发展管理法中制定的加强交通机动性的相同内容。

1991年通过的《综合地面交通效率法案》(简称ISTEA,谐音"冰茶")使交通拨款提高了近一倍；设立了用于行人和自行车交通设施以及强化其他交通方式的专项资金；允许公路建设资金用于其他用途；提供新的资金以用于减轻空气污染地区的交通堵塞问题。然而,ISTEA并不如预期的那样具有革命性,部分原因是缺少充分的资金支持,还有一部分原因是做出拨款决定的是与ISTEA之前相同的政府和当地机构,如今的交通投资却比以往任何时候都更加平衡[16]。

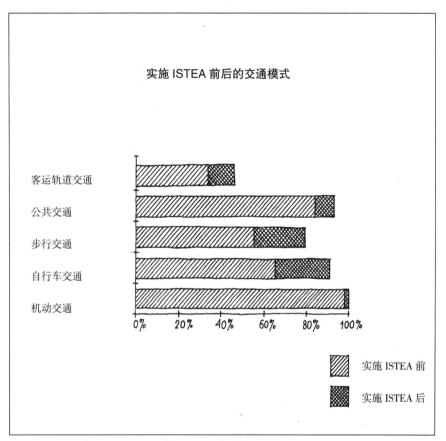

图片来源：引自T.L. Shaw的《ISTEA对大都市规划实践的影响》,交通工程师学会（ITE）1996年科技论文汇编,交通工程师协会,华盛顿哥伦比亚特区,1996年。©1996年交通工程师协会,已获授权使用。

ISTEA 需要因地制宜，在交通管理地区（拥有 20 万及以上人口的城市化地区）建立交通堵塞管理系统和覆盖全国范围各州的均衡的系统。无论面积是大是小，佛罗里达州的所有城市化地区都已经超出了 ISTEA 规定的拥堵管理系统要求，并基本满足了联邦政府作为"机动性"规定的要求[17]。转变必须是综合措施的一部分，需要大力鼓励自行车出行、步行和交通需求管理措施。再次强调，一系列的措施包括了许多与早前佛罗里达州 1993 年的城市发展管理法中制定的加强交通机动性相同的内容。

ISTEA 于 1997 年重新获得授权，尽管有关于"热茶"（在强调公路建设的时期，仅有交通拨款）和"温茶"（整笔拨款无条件划拨各州），但人们确信现行的法律将会进行适当调整并得到强化。

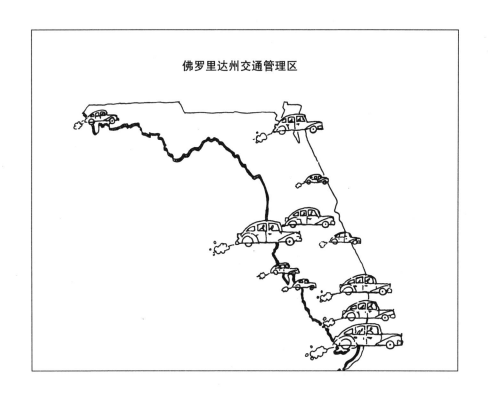

佛罗里达州交通管理区

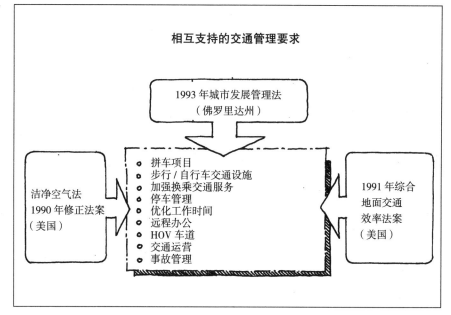

相互支持的交通管理要求

第三章 机动性规划要素

近期相关法律规定的变化显示了政策方面的转变,也是理念初步转变的一个信号。奥兰多市的综合规划及其实施进程,清晰地阐释了实践的新思路,并作为实例在本章中加以分析。

1 远景规划

远景规划可以让官员感受到社会的脉搏,也就是说,要找出真正的问题所在,并以市民的视角来看待问题。

华盛顿州社会发展部[18]

佛罗里达本地的综合规划重在现状分析和远景目标。随着佛罗里达州1993年城市发展管理法的通过,远景规划被作为综合规划进程的一部分加以鼓励和推广[19]。

在远景规划中,力求就城市未来的发展目标达成共识,并制定相应的规划以实现这一目标[20]。远景规划并不是过分强调技术层面,更多的是讨论理念和价值,而非数据分析。通常情况下,要对未来提出几个可能的预想,并从中选择最终的发展目标。所选择的远景以图纸或图片等可视化手段展示,以帮助参与者对未来有直观的感知。还要以配合图片及说明文字的多媒体方式,展现规划远景。

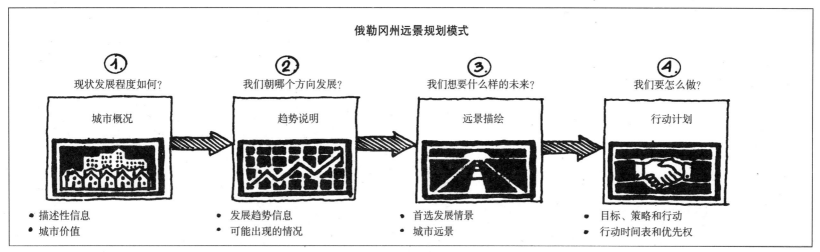

资料来源:S·C·埃姆斯主编,社会远景发展目标指导,俄勒冈州远景规划,俄勒冈章节,美国规划协会,1993年。©1992 史蒂文·C·埃姆斯

远景规划的制定要举办公共论坛。社会群体领导者，利益集团代表，和其他"利益相关者"被邀请参加讨论。尽管可能会由专业人员完成技术部分的内容，但参与者可制定目标和实施计划，以实现未来发展。若要制定一个得到整个社会和城市管理者都认同的远景规划，那么这个阶段的公众参与是必不可少的。

与上述例子相似的远景规划的案例遍布佛罗里达。具有代表性的有《萨拉索塔2020》《2010城市形态——棕榈滩县远景规划》和《沃卢斯亚远景规划》。在奥兰多，各种可能的未来图景展现在社会群体领导者面前。未来的主要活动中心将有内部交通系统，并以公交车和拼车专用车道连接外部公路，相关集团对于这样的远景规划表示欢迎。奥兰多综合规划将给出这一远景规划的形式和内容。

2 土地利用规划

> 机动性真正指的是到达目的地的能力。换句话说，可达性是关键，而不是所使用的交通工具。
>
> 贝弗利·沃德[21]

就像所有的交通入门课程所强调的那样，交通需求是一种派生需求。也就是说，交通在很大程度上是一种人们出行的手段，而非人们出行的目的，如果交通有目的的话，应该这样认为：人们可以很便利地到外面从事活动，并且可以很方便地回家，出行的可达性高，这是再好不过的了。

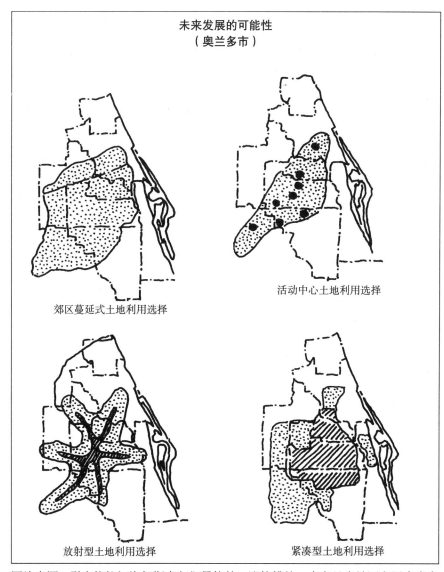

图片来源：引自格拉汀洛佩斯克尔彻昂格林，迎接挑战：大奥兰多地区交通未来发展共识，大奥兰多商会，1989年。

如果交通距离变短，步行和自行车成为可行的出行选择，单一出行可以完成多重目的，而多个目的间穿梭的机动交通可以变得更加高效[22]。

佛罗里达州长期以来一直在寻求促进紧凑发展、综合利用的城市中心，城市化的乡村和自给自足的新城镇。1994年的行政法规抑制了城市的蔓延，鼓励了上述地区的发展[23]。

土地的综合利用和提高可达性的簇群发展，是这种更加紧凑的城市发展模式与佛罗里达普遍存在的蔓延式发展的区别。优秀的土地利用规划所具备的特点：混合利用，地区、社区和活动中心三个层面的簇群发展。据估计，车辆行驶里程（VMT）将较城市蔓延发展时减少一半，而新的发展规划正满足了这一要求[24]。

现在，城市发展模式随着时间的推移慢慢地发生了变化，这已成为不争的事实。即便如此，在佛罗里达州高增速的发展模式下，紧凑发展可以在一个长期规划的20年左右，使地区内的车辆行驶里程（VMT）减少百分之十以上（相对于城市蔓延发展）[25]。同时，所取得的任何形式的减少将持续多年，主要是由于相应的基础设施和建筑，都具有相同的寿命长的性质，这就使得将改变发展模式放在首要地位变得困难。

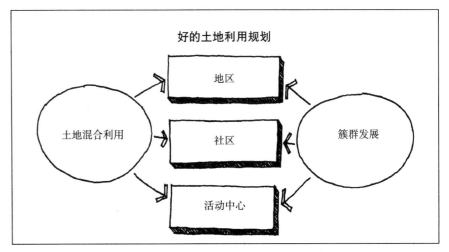

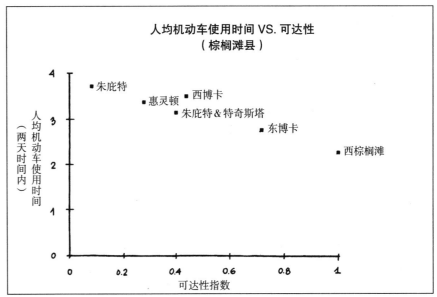

图片来源：R·尤因，P·哈里尤拉，G·W·佩奇，传统城市周边，郊区发展单元规划和两者间的交通问题，交通运输研究记录1466，交通运输研究委员会，华盛顿哥伦比亚特区，1994年。

同样，以奥兰多为例，它的综合规划引导城市向综合利用的活动中心和廊道发展。这些中心和廊道必须满足某种最低密度标准，以便居住、办公、商业和公共利用几种用地功能达到综合平衡。

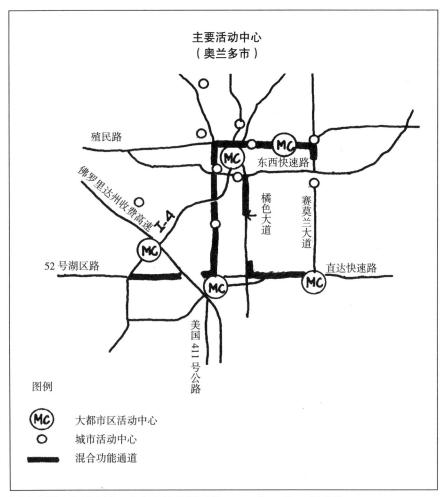

图片来源：奥兰多城，未来土地利用要素，1991年8月12日获批。

3 路网设计

相较于分布着高等级道路的相同街区，小尺度相互连接的路网具有更高的交通容量……街区面积增大应该带来规模效益，相反，我们所体会到的是由于规模扩张所带来的不经济。

沃尔特·库拉西[26]

作为一项课题，由于工程与规划之间联系的断裂，道路路网设计并未受到重视。然而，有证据表明，像土地利用一样，路网结构对于城市交通具有重要影响[27]。

根据佛罗里达州1993年的城市发展管理法，只有街道路网为居民提供多种交通可能性的地区，才有资格成为TCMAs。这一规定是因为其特殊的地位而制定的。为疏导交通、避免交通堵塞，街道路网必须为各人流活动中心之间提供多种交通连接。为鼓励步行、自行车交通和换乘交通，路网必须提供合理而直接的交通路线。曲折且连续性差的道路也可满足时速在35英里/小时的汽车的交通需求，但对于速度在3英里/小时的行人来说，这样的道路太长了。这样的道路迫使公交车路线单一，且交通目的性差，很难在步行交通范围内为居民提供有效的交通服务。

没有人鼓吹永无止境的笔直的方格网道路系统。短而弯曲绵延，遵循地形变化或者有助于良好城市设计的道路系统是好的。所以，只要是合理布局的路网，即使是小环路和尽端路也能提供更多的相互联系和交通。

高等级道路（主干路、次干路和支路）之间的间距不应超过半英里，不规则的道路路网也应采用与此相近的路网密度。这将有效提高过境交通的效率，缩短街区之间的交通，减缓六车道或八车道这样的重要交通通道的通行压力[28]。

在奥兰多市的综合规划中，新的居住用地必须满足一定的道路条件："地块与周边的开发地区要有连续的交通联系，以满足相邻邻里单位间的交通需求……"。新的居住地块必须为居民提供与邻近学校、社区中心和商业地段直接的步行和自行车交通联系。

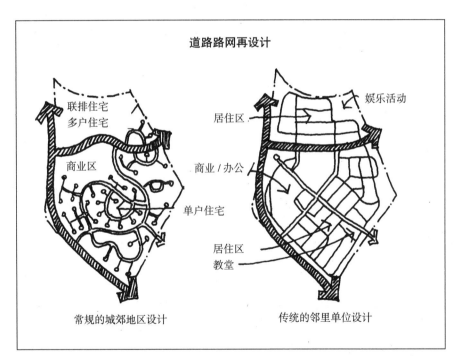

图片来源：M·J·韦尔斯，新传统邻里单位发展：你又可以回家了，作者尚未发表论文，韦尔斯及合作者公司，阿灵顿，弗吉尼亚州，1993年。

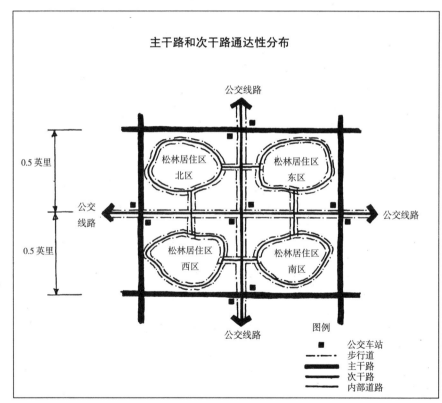

图片来源：丹佛地区政府委员会，郊区机动交通设计手册，丹佛，科罗拉多州，1993年。

4 城市设计

……设计师的首要任务是创造一定的空间，将人们从私密空间引导出来……

安德烈斯·杜安伊，伊丽莎白·普拉特—齐贝克[29]

城市设计与规划在尺度规模、定位、空间的处理上存在差别。设计的尺度主要是指道路、停车场、换乘站大小的规模，而不是较大的地区、居住社区或者大的活动中心。在定位方面，设计是一个广义的美学概念，介于以美为目的的艺术和以功能为目的的规划之间；在空间处理方面，设计是一种三维空间的思考，在街道空间、停车场空间和其他城市空间的设计中，竖向要素与横向要素同样重要。与之相反，规划则是一种二维的活动（如图所示，以平面图的方式呈现）[30]。

很多评论已经指出，像城市一样，佛罗里达州的许多郊区缺乏很好的城市设计。毫无疑问，这提高了居民对汽车的依赖程度。研究指出，以行人为设计导向比以机动车为设计导向的地区，步行、自行车和换乘交通的利用率更高[31]。

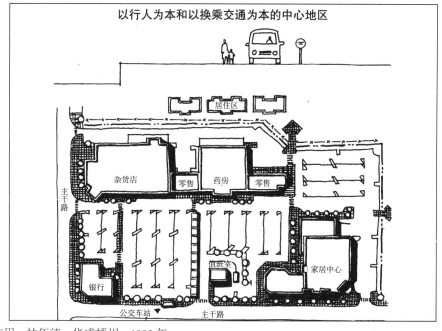

图片来源：斯诺霍米什县交通运输管理局，土地利用和公共交通规划导则；第二卷：概念应用，林伍德，华盛顿州，1993年。

直到最近，城郊规划更像是一个矛盾混合体而不是一个成熟的领域。时代在变化，一批设计师倡导传统的小城镇规划，在他们看来，佛罗里达州的城郊地区是领导"新传统主义"的大本营，也是被广泛认同的新传统式发展和滨水胜地规划的成功案例[32]。另外一些设计师团体提倡城郊围绕城市的口袋式发展，都市地区周围围绕着低密度的郊区。提出"步行口袋"这一概念的设计师指出，他的心血结晶——博卡拉顿的米兹纳公园是佛罗里达州发展过程中已建成的案例[33]。另外的一些设计师正努力使城郊中心和次中心、购物中心等成为独立的设计内容，使其更具吸引力，更加适合步行[34]。

城市也好，城郊也罢，从之前的讨论看出，好的设计必须是以行人为本的。以行人为本具有以下几个特点：人行尺度（小尺度）的街区、道路、建筑、停车场和指示标志；建筑退线适中，且建筑间距适宜，从视觉上产生围合街道的效果；可达的和形式多样的公共空间；与建筑入口直接连通的连续步道；沿街立面采用柱廊、拱廊和门廊等设计要素；通过行道树、檐棚和其他出挑结构提供庇荫场所；增加中央步道、拐角、连接的步行通道和其他步行通道辅助方式；利用邻近街道的窗户、隐藏的车库和低矮的墙体和灌木，使街道边缘"透明"，增加视线的通透性；还有水景小品、公共艺术品、特殊的铺装材料和其他一些具有场所特点的"场所营造者"。这些特点将在第八章（以行人和自行车交通为本的设计）进行更充分的讨论。

我们所分析的案例——奥兰多，是佛罗里达州少数几个可以将城市设计要素纳入综合规划的城市之一。设计要素将奥兰多中心区和其周边的邻里单位，划定为"传统城市"。采用特殊的城市设计标准，沿街进行建设，减小建筑退线距离和路段间距，禁止枯燥的立面设计和柱式的指示系统，加入停车场和停车库的设计，以及与主要人行道的步行连接。

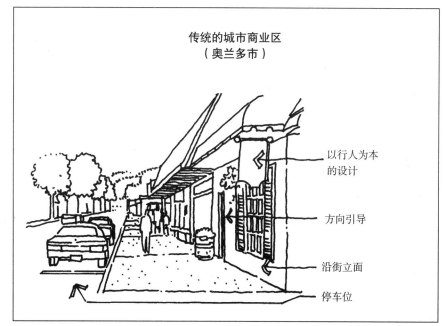

图片来源：奥兰多城，土地开发保护编码和建筑设计实施图示。

15

5　交通工具

那些正在努力"缓解交通堵塞"的人就好像是一个手里仅仅拿着一个小斧头，却必须砍倒一棵大树的伐木工人一样。他无法伐倒一棵树，甚至每次挥动斧头都没有什么作用。但最终，靠着成百次的反复砍伐，他还是能砍倒一个大树。

安东尼·唐斯[35]

一部关于机动性的文献很好地介绍了缓解交通堵塞的"工具"，我们将借用其中的一部分[36]。文章对机动性工具进行了详细的阐述，在如此浩繁的手册中，这一部分被亲切地称为"电话簿"。我们不想复制这些很好的阐述。后面的章节将简单梳理一下最有前景的集中工具和方法，看看它们用在什么地方是有效的，如何做才能使它们更加有效。

近20年来，许多新的研究已量化了个人交通工具对于交通、交通堵塞、尾气排放和燃料消耗的影响[37]。一般来说，个人交通工具将造成1%~2%的影响，少数可能会达到5%~10%。例如，专家们认为拼车上班可以缓解地区3%～5%的通勤交通[38]。当交通量的增速达到每年3%~5%时，这就不能奏效了。

因此，一个机动性规划必须依靠多样化的方法措施，以实现大范围的积累影响。这些方法措施必须适合于交通环境，必须相互补充和结合，而不是削弱彼此的影响。

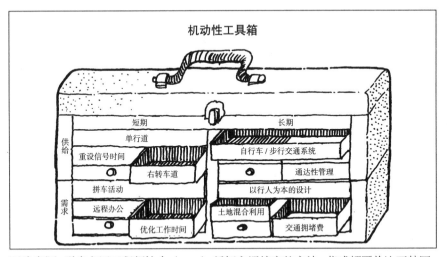

图片来源：引自交通工程师协会（ITE），缓解交通堵塞的方法，华盛顿哥伦比亚特区，1989年。©1989交通工程师协会，已获授权使用。

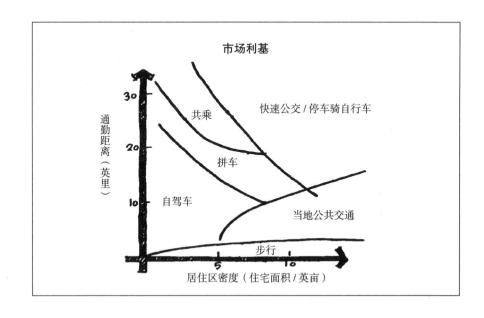

同样，以奥兰多综合规划为例，大都市地区的活动中心必须有内部的公交和步行系统、高效的换乘系统和各自的交通管理协会以推广拼车和错开高峰时段的上下班时间。上述这些举措配合高密度的路网和土地的混合利用，以提高机动车的利用率并倡导机动车使用者改用其他交通方式。

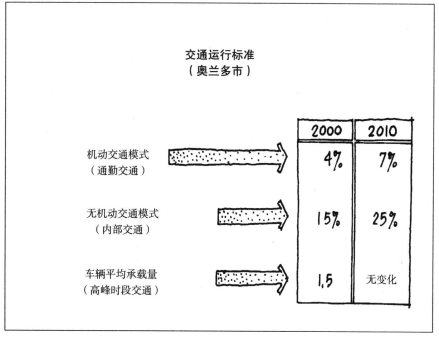

图片来源：奥兰多城，交通运输要素，1991年8月12日获批；交通线路要素，1991年8月12日获批。

第四章 基于可达性的土地规划

……增加城市的机动性也许根本不是需要更多的交通，而可能更多的是要依赖于像区位、决策和美学等这类非交通的方式综合考虑，以满足城市居民的需求。

威尔弗雷德·欧文[39]

威尔弗雷德·欧文在其经典著作《可达性城市》(The Accessible City)中将当代的城市地区比作设计不佳的建筑。如果一个医院的交通流线被设计成连运送食物都要穿过手术室的话，这将导致交通流量的增大和使用效率的降低。同时，一个好的医院设计要有相应的活动安排规划，以减少不必要的流动和避免那些不必要的交通穿越。这一原则同样适用于一个规划良好的城市地区。

随着其他提高机动性措施的局限性更加明显，交通问题专家对土地利用规划越来越感兴趣。这不是因为土地利用规划在今天的美国得到了实践，政府也将其作为对开发商建议的回应，而是因为积极的土地利用规划可以成为政府寻求缓解大量机动交通需求的手段。尽管有一些思想已经根深蒂固，但是佛罗里达州城市发展管理进程的重点已经从保证道路交通的服务水平转到了遏制城市蔓延上（详见第二、三、九章）。

从不同角度来看可达性

家庭交通出行是一个关于可达性的函数。户外活动目的地与居住地的邻近程度，即所谓的"居住可达性"，会影响家庭出行的距离、模式，甚至可以说，会影响家庭出游的频率[40]。另一种可达性则较少受到关注，

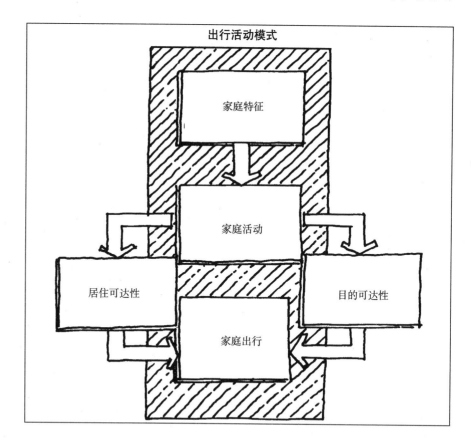

但却也非常重要。目的地的可达性,即不同的户外活动目的地之间的邻近程度会影响出行者将短途出行有效地连接成长途出行的能力,或者最好是仅停留一次便可完成不止一项的活动[41]。"一个邻近决策者工作地的商店的可达性可能会很高(按使用频率计算),即使它可能距离决策者居住地很远"[42]。

机动车使用者仅仅承担了机动交通的经济和社会总成本的一部分(详见第一章)。无可厚非的是,相对于出行成本,他们更多的是关注土地、住房和消费品成本(占大部分家庭预算)。因此,政府有责任通过积极的土地利用规划使可达性成为土地功能布局的优先考虑因素,而不能指望私人市场去做这些事情。

区域

我们所关注的土地规划中的最大地理单位通常是区域。区域规划的重点是工作通勤,我们想尽可能缩短个人通勤距离,同时引导单人通勤向拼车以及使用换乘交通方式的转变。为此,城市必须承载发展需求而不是无休止地向外蔓延,就业岗位须集中在几个中心城区,并在一些次级区域内达到职居平衡[43]。

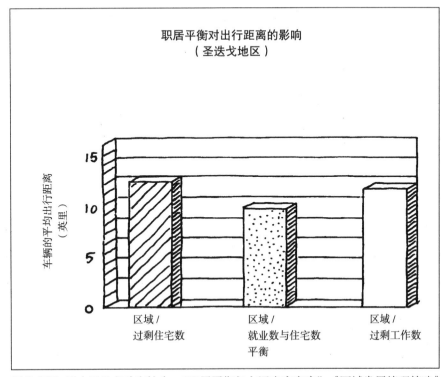

图片来源:引自圣迭戈政府协会,"职居平衡与交通走廊密度",《区域发展管理策略》附录3、圣迭戈、加利福尼亚州、1991年。

我们可以从国际研究中发现,拥有单一主导功能的高密度城市区域有可能拥有最小的车辆行驶里程(VMT)。许多出行目的地都在步行可达范围之内,公共交通可以提供很好的到市中心的通勤服务,机动交通的使用也因中心区的停车和交通堵塞问题而受到了限制。机动车的使用仅限于相对的短途交通,并可能起到有效的交通连接作用。不同的估算结果表明，当城市密度提高一倍时，车辆行驶里程（VMT）将减少 25% ~ 30%，即使其他影响因素受到控制时，VMT 也会有小幅度的减少[44]。

然而，随着城市面积的不断增加，中心城市变得越来越不容易向边缘地区发展。其他主要中心区的涌现在某种程度上或许是得益于交通站点的建设。相比就业集中的中心——商务中心区，多中心模式采用的是分散式交通，就业者可以选择靠近工作地点的地区居住[45]。

一些研究已经对其他的区域发展模式进行了比较[46]。一些模式通过建设副中心，以取得职居平衡；另一些模式是在区域性的城市核心区或一些主要中心区提供多样化的就业岗位；还有一些模式是将就业集中于众多的小型中心区。

综合考虑交通堵塞问题和车辆行驶里程（VMT），最佳模式是适度地集中发展一些地区（不是过度发展）并在更小的区域内达到职居平衡。这种结合的发展模式通过提高出行速度和减少了区域内车辆行驶里程（VMT），提供了最好、最全面的可达性。

发展模式对交通出行影响

	集中就业	聚集居住	混合土地使用	VMT（%）变化率	行驶速度（%）变化率
华盛顿特区					
平衡		○	●	-9	+1
集中	●	○	●	-9	+2
西雅图					
主要中心区	●	●		-4	-7
多中心区	○		●	-1	0
分散发展			○	+3	0
首选替代	●	●		-3	+7
米德尔塞克斯					
情境 1	●	●	○	-12	+21
情境 2	○	○	○	-9	+11
达拉斯沃斯堡					
铁路交通走廊	●	●	○	-1	-2
活动中心	●			-1	0
非交通堵塞区域			○	-4	+2

图例：

就业
● 高度集中
○ 低度集中

住房
● 高度聚集
○ 低度聚集

土地利用
● 职居平衡
○ 职居混合

图片来源：R·尤因。《关于城市扩张的特征、原因和影响的文献综述》环境和城市问题，第 21 卷，1994 年第四季度。

弗吉尼亚州的劳顿县、马里兰州的蒙哥马利县和俄勒冈州的波特兰是很好的区域规划案例。每个成功的案例都采用了各自独特的方式进行紧凑发展。佛罗里达州塔拉哈西地区的都市规划机构比较了三种土地利用方案。方案一是城市向东和东北部扩张发展，方案二是集中于城市区域进行高密度发展，方案三是在尚未充分开发的东南部地区进行综合社区开发。拥有最少的交通堵塞路段和车辆行驶里程（VMT）的方案受到了青睐并最终被采纳[47]。两名可以充分代表都市规划组织的地方官员均来自塔拉哈西地区，因此，通过修改本地的综合规划来实施最佳方案变得十分容易。

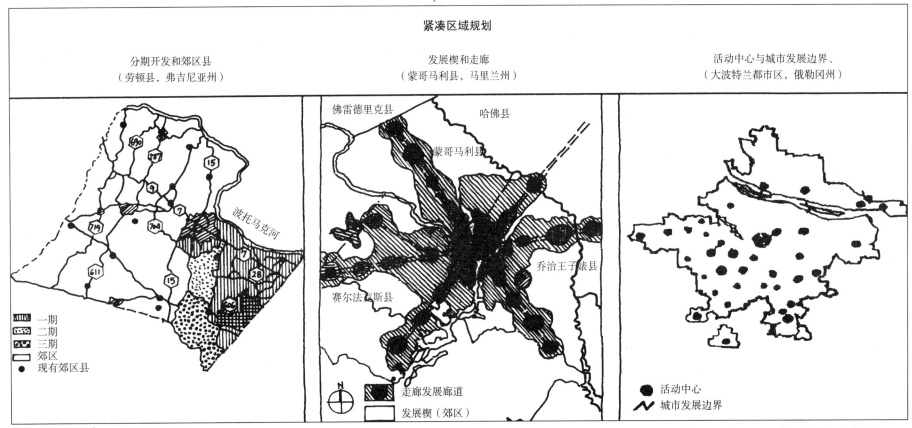

图片来源：劳顿县规划署、劳顿县总体规划。1991年9月17日获批。蒙哥马利县规划细则——楔形绿地与绿色廊道的目标与宗旨，蒙哥马利县，1992年。波特兰都市区"2040发展设想"，2040都市区发展框架更新。春/夏季。1995年。

社区

现在，我们将研究范围从区域转移到地区内的单个社区。社区规划的重点在于居民的购物、娱乐和上学等出行的便利性。相对于其他购物或就医出行，这些出行活动更频繁且更容易受到可达性的影响[48]。

我们的目标是将这些出行活动尽可能地排除在区域城市路网的辐射之外。如果出行距离足够短，有些出行活动就可以通过步行或骑自行车来完成。

过去，新建社区经常呈现蜂窝式的布局，细胞式的邻里单位拥有各自的商业中心和内部休闲设施[49]。从服务的效率、公共选择和社区凝聚力这些角度来看，这种划分是不必要和不可取的[50]。相反，服务设施最好布置在邻里单位内部和邻里单位之间，以便使社区内部紧密联系在一起，这是对居住与非居住的土地利用预期相互作用的结果。

计算机模拟研究表明，混合功能的社区在减少车辆行驶里程（VMT）、出行时间和道路交叉口延误等方面具有一定潜力[51]。对新传统主义社区进行的设计研究表明，设计者已经开始将土地细分成小地块（这些地块的大小与土地利用功能单一时相同）进行土地功能的混合利用，并通过简单的网状道路系统划分（"网格"是典型的街道空间）保证合理直接的交通通行。即便是在以机动交通为设计导向的社区，网状道路系统使

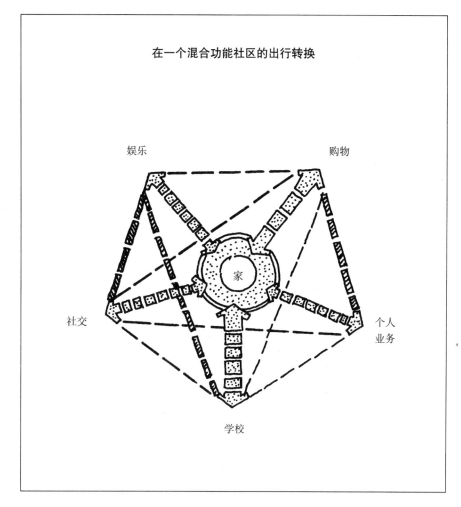

区域内的购物、去公园或学校等出行距离在很大程度上有所减少，并最终缩短了车辆行驶里程（VMT）[52]。

棕榈滩县新传统主义分区条例规定，社区附近的购物地点，托儿所和市政建筑均应在住宅的 1320 英尺范围内，邻里公园应在 600 英尺范围内；城镇中心可以提供一些额外的购物机会。一个新传统主义社区不仅要"平衡"内部的土地用途，而且它必须有助于平衡该县各部分的工作、住房和可用的开放空间。

出行可以在没有新传统主义或任何其他设计形式的帮助下内部化。希尔斯堡县为"计划村"提供了土地开发的秘诀，最低目标是集群发展、就地工作、购物和内部出行，相应地，由地块增加所带来的增量也会最小化。在超过一半的住房建立起来以前，必须构建好一半的商业和办公空间，这样就业和购物才能跟得上人口发展。

有趣的是，任何一个创新条例都没有进展，原因之一是大规模的开发建设不是经常出现的；另一个原因是当地太容易开发无关的住宅小区、购物中心和商业公园。这需要我们重拾有前瞻性的土地规划的概念，而不是允许每个开发人员自己决定做什么，地方必须开始整合个人的土地储备成为统一的居住区、村庄、社区。他们必须也开始提供容积率奖励、影响费折扣、加快审批等激励措施来鼓励这些发展。

马里兰州，霍华德县的混合利用地区条例就是一个很好的例子。根据该条例的比例进行土地混合利用，大量土地所有者可以制定并提交一份符合自身特点及周边需求的区域范围内的发展计划，周边地区发展也要与之配合。大型土地所有者及其周边地区开发者可以合作制定更为集约的发展计划，一经采用，则用于整个地区的开发者。这个计划必须包括商业以及住宅用地，混合的住宅类型，至少 35% 的开放空间，和一个开发重点，比如通过一个城市广场来统一开发。

"规划乡村"的需求（希尔斯堡县）

	乡村规模			
	160-320 英亩	320-640 英亩	640-2560 英亩	+2560 英亩
本地出行需求				
工作机会	15%	25%	40%	55%
邻里单位购物中心	50%	75%	100%	100%
社区购物中心	—	—	25%	50%
本地出行的百分比	12%	16%	20%	24%

图片来源：希尔斯堡县，土地开发准则，坦帕，佛罗里达州。

活动中心

混合土地利用的最小单位是城市或郊区的活动中心。虽然活动中心有时包括居住功能，它在结合零售、办公、娱乐和公共使用等方面有很大潜力。从交通角度来看，如果出行目的地有足够的可达性，即使是自驾出行，也可以在其中通过步行来达到多种出行目的。

以一个城市的市中心作为出行目的地可达性的代表来说，在市中心区，工作的人不需要开车就可以完成许多任务。以一个区域性的购物中心作为另外一个代表，购物者在这样的环境中仅停留一次，便可步行完成多项活动。在其他的就业及购物中心，我们也想尽可能地建立这样的区域。

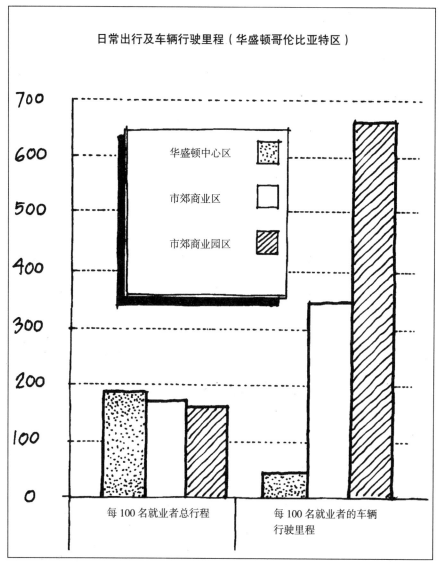

图片来源：G·B·道格拉斯，"土地利用模式对市郊机动性的影响"，年会宣讲论文，交通工程师协会，华盛顿哥伦比亚特区，1992年。

我们可以通过"高密度"活动中心的建设和就业与购物相结合的出行活动来达到这一目的[53]。银行、餐馆、便利店、卡片店和健身俱乐部是员工中午最常去的地方；那些杂货店、银行、干洗店、餐厅和学校或日托中心是人们在上班前后最常去的地方[54]。在购物中心，即便是小规模的混合利用，与平日单一的出行相比，也可以减少25%的出行距离[55]。在商业公园，地区内所提供的服务种类和购物机会可使职员的车辆行驶里程（VMT）减少20%[56]。

高密度的中心区和混合性的活动将有另一个有益的作用——鼓励他们使用替代性的交通模式，因为员工在上班前、上班时和上班后对机动车的需求都会降低。在通勤调查中，使用汽车的主要原因之一是需要停车或在途中观光旅行[57]。员工拼车出行、步行或骑自行车和使用公共交通去郊区的就业中心上班的比例将会因土地利用功能的混合使用而上升[58]。

佛罗里达州地区的许多综合规划都对于活动中心作出了明确的说明。坦帕湾指定了四种类型的活动中心，波尔克县有八种。奥兰多则更进一步，已经开始降低住宅密度，降低容积率并减少活动中心各种功能用地所占的比例，以此来减少人们对机动车的依赖。

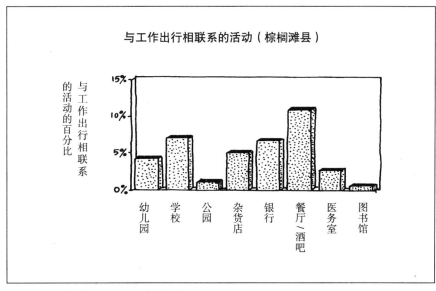

图片来源：家庭出行调查，棕榈滩县，5/91－7/91。

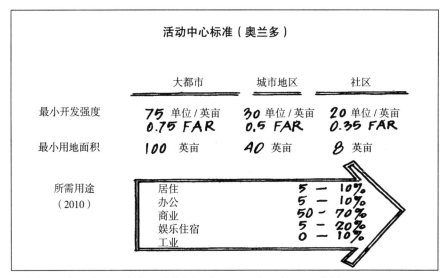

图片来源：奥兰多城，未来土地使用要素，1991年8月12日获批。

第五章　交通需求管理

关于交通行为研究的采集对象是明确的，这表明交通行为确实随着出行者面临情况不同而有很大差别，另外不同的政策也会导致不同的选择。

马丁·瓦克斯[59]

时间回溯到1984年，地点是由于交通拥堵而声名狼藉的洛杉矶。为了迎接即将到来的奥运会，这里将有120万人次游客，大约25000名运动员，媒体和粉丝蜂拥而至，市长因此而倍感焦虑。令人倍感意外的是当奥运会开幕之后交通竟然井然有序甚至比往常还要畅通。究竟是怎样神奇的魔法使得交通如此顺畅？其实并不存在魔法，仅仅是一个关于交通需求管理和机动性措施的前所未有的承诺，类似的承诺在佛罗里达或者其他任何地方都没有出现过，并且还存在很大的提升空间。

没有什么新奇的或者再看看？

TDM（Travel Demand Management）可能会让人联想起一个由电脑产生的陌生人名单，你可以和这些陌生人拼车但是你却不希望这么做。这种私下的地区性的拼车活动并不是今天才出现的，早在20世纪70年代已经很普遍。现在TDM很大程度上依赖雇主、财政和其他激励措施，针对不同的市场还会有不同的策略。目前的发展现状在最近的出版物中都有涉及[60]。

雇主发起的TDM还有很大的改进空间

策略	雇主感兴趣的可能性	目前的可行性
为拼车提供匹配列表	34%	2%
提供交通情况简报	32%	-
错峰上下班15分钟到2个小时	30%	13%
为拼车提供有限停车	26%	-
激励拼车行为	23%	-
提供弹性时间	23%	11%
降低合伙拼车的停车费用	22%	-
自行车出行	21%	7%
压缩周工作时间（40h/4天）	19%	4%
容许远程办公	19%	10%
补贴公共汽车执照	19%	2%

图片来源：奥兰多市中心区交通管理协会，奥兰多市中心通勤情况调查。奥兰多，佛罗里达州，1991年。

相比运输和绿色出行来说，TDM 在降低居住密度方面更有成效。这对于肆意蔓延的佛罗里达无疑是一个好消息。拼车或者班车只适用于家庭住址和工作单位一致的中密度家庭。由于浪费在接其他乘客的时间被通勤本身的真正成本节约所抵消，长时间的通勤实际上有助于交通共享。

弹性工作时间、错开工作时间、缩短工作周很好地切合了那些交通拥堵仅仅在早晨和下午短时间发生的人口中低密度的区域。即使稍微调整一下工作时间也可以很好的避开乘客上下班的高峰期。

由于员工可以通过通信技术以光速与办公室进行交流，电子办公就变得和居住密度毫无关系。约束远程办公的是工作本身而不是工作的地点。当然只有适宜信息化办公的人才和工作岗位是我们讨论的对象，不过，这也涵盖了将近一半的员工，并且这一比例还在持续增加。

雇主的重要作用

雇主是交通需求管理模式成功的关键一环。他们有规定工作时间和建立信息化办公的权利，他们可以为那些拼车的人提供财政支持或者其他奖励。他们可以雇佣交通协调员制定个性化的员工通勤，进行员工远程办公培训，并开展公用拼车上下班行动。

通过制定协议或者法规，建立交通管理协会，或者减少行程条例，可能调动员工的积极性[61]。协议或者法规是在开发者或者继承者有特殊

迪士尼新城（奥兰多地区）发展进程中 TDM 的需求	Required	Encouraged
交通管理协会	✓	
拼车协调员	✓	
拼车信息展示	✓	
为拼车提供优先停车位	✓	
公共汽车候车厅 / 公交港湾式停靠站	✓	
为员工提供交通收费折扣	✓	
内部公交系统		✓
酒店巴士	✓	
自行车专用道 / 自行车停车位	✓	
为骑车上下班的员工提供冲凉条件		✓
即停即用自行车租赁点	✓	
机动性的工作时间		✓

行为的情况下达成的，但是道路改善却普遍需要。TDM 管理措施现在出现在一些发展迅速的法规里，尤其是在地方规划局可以大展拳脚的奥兰多。

TMA 是由雇主为了协调 TDM 项目而成立的组织。他们为自己的成员提供拼车匹配服务、乘车折扣、班车服务，并执行其他与机动性相关的功能。佛罗里达有 11 个 TMA，并通过在西佛罗里达大学的 TMA 交流中心为他们提供配套资金和技术支持。

TROs 是地方性条款，规定雇主必须在高峰时段减少出入所在地点的车次。虽然 TDM 措施通常是供雇主选择的，但节能减排的目标仍是为他们设置的。如果他们不能达到这一目标，雇主必须给员工提供更多的激励直到达到目标。截止到 1996 年年末佛罗里达已经有 2 个 TROs（分别是在迈阿密和博卡拉顿）。第三个在西棕榈滩的市中心筹建中，以作为交通税务减免中心。（详见第二章关于佛罗里达州发展管理法的讨论）。

佛罗里达的 TMAs/TMOs

- 大学 – 阿拉法亚 – 走廊（奥兰多）
- 西海岸（坦帕湾）
- 奥兰多市中心
- 首府城市（塔拉哈西）
- 劳德尔堡市中心
- 坦帕市中心
- 西棕榈滩
- 市民中心（迈阿密）
- 南部海岸（迈阿密）
- 圣彼得堡市中心
- 南佛罗里达教育中心（佛罗里达州，劳德尔堡）

快速发展对 TRO 的要求
（迈阿密中心城区）

● 高峰时段车流量下降 10%

● 减少员工出行计划

● 拼车上下班咨询服务

● 交通路线

● 公共候车站与周转路线

● 成果年报

第四个为塔拉哈西地区设立的TRO过去一直在筹建中，但至今仍未实施。如果在塔拉哈西区关于TDM的强制性要求已应用于所有雇主，大约有4%~15%的高峰时段的车流量已经被削减[62]。一个自愿的或者一个只是为了新发展而制定的强制措施所带来的后果和作用是显而易见的[63]。

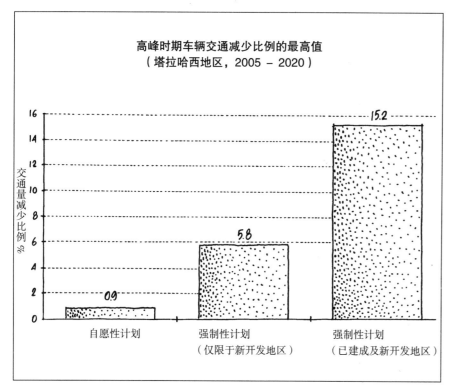

图片来源：波斯特，巴克利，舒和杰公司，交通需求管理计划——结题报告，塔拉哈西-立昂县都市规划组织，塔拉哈西，佛罗里达州，1994年。

将权利授予雇主一直饱受争议，以至于国会拒绝了一个臭氧污染极端严重地区的雇主的雇员出行申请，以洛杉矶地区做估算[64]，事实上，就目前做最乐观的估计，与其他减少车辆行程与汽车尾气排放的措施相比，减少雇员出行这一措施表现出一定的竞争力[65]。

停车场的重要作用

大多数雇主为雇员和访客在靠近入口的地区提供了免费的足够的停车空间。雇员独自驾车上班前往各自的停车位停车是很常见的。

大量的免费停车可能是一个简单的市场运作的结果，如果没有与其对手匹敌的停车空间，办公园区或者购物中心到底如何争夺雇员或者顾客（甚至银行金融）？

事实上政府政策已经有助于创造令人向往的停车空间。政府一直将对雇员的停车补助视为不受限制的税务，然而，补助一旦超过一定的数量，对于交通使用者的税收便会增加，免费停车位依然比其他形式的雇员补助有更多的税收优惠[66]。

土地开发对停车位的控制仍然是规模最小值，路边停车位的需求远远超过正常的发展需要。在郊区办公地带，停车供给已经超过需求高峰的30%或更多[67]。

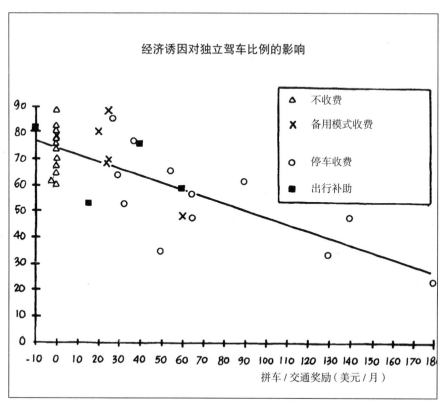

图片来源：G·S·卢瑟福等《交通需求管理——中型企业的案例研究》交通研究记录 1459. 交通研究委员会，全美研究会，华盛顿哥伦比亚特区，1994年。

停车费限制停车已被证明可以最有效地鼓励拼车[68]，个人通勤时间通过建立市场化的停车收费机制可以减少20%或更多[69]。如果停车成本是他们日常花销的一部分，雇员有强大的动力去拼车或者使用公共交通工具，如果拼车可以免费停车或有停车费优惠，而单独驾驶则要收全额停车费，那么拼车将变得更有吸引力。

为了克服员工的阻力，雇主可以采用交通补贴和停车收费并用的方式，即使自驾车出行的员工可以支付成本，拼车的员工仍可获得一定的补偿[70]。此外，雇主可为员工提供选择免费停车位或等价的交通条件或公共交通补贴。所谓的"兑现"停车补贴，这项政策的局限是仅适用于所有在加利福尼亚州的大型企业[71]。一项评估显示，在被提供代替现金支付停车补贴的情况下，13%的员工转变了独自出行而选择其他方式[72]。如上所述，美国气候变化行动计划也包含一个限制现金补贴的行动[73]。

对于地方政府来说，他们可以协助雇主更改土地开发模式来平衡停车供需关系，甚至令停车位供应略显紧张。如果土地开发结合不同的停车形式，则可获得一定的贷款，这样的做法在佛罗里达州很少使用[74]，不断改进的停车政策在一些技术导则里已有概述[75]。

前进式停车场需求		
（每1000平方英尺的所需空间）		
	Minimum	Maximum
城市中心	2	2.5
其他主要城市活动中心	2.5	3
其他地区	2.5	4
☆ 标准适用于大多数办公楼、商店及服务设施		

图片来源：奥兰多市，土地开发准则，1993年获批。

其他拼车奖励措施

大量免费的停车位遍布佛罗里达的大部分地区，这可能说明收取停车费不切实际（甚至抵消了出行补助）[76]。接下来要做的事最好是为拼车出行、公共交通出行、步行和自行车出行提供积极的奖励措施，奖励措施可以各式各样，现金奖励历来是很好的方式（并且是唯一一条绝对可以影响到雇员的措施）[77]。额外的优惠停车时间、有安全保证的骑车回家、在公司食堂免费就餐等是其中的一小部分，为了实现出行减排要求，雇主可以提供各式奖励。

比公共出行更加实惠的方法

在今天高速运转的生活模式下，我们唯一能停下来不工作的时间可能就是通勤的时候。我们都不情愿花额外的时间去接送陌生人或者偶遇的搭车人，也会在上下班路上顺便做些其他事情[78]。以上这些原因使得公共出行变得叫好不叫座，并使得财政奖励成为必然选择。

经过调整的工作时间和远程办公却不是这样。他们本身有足够的吸引力，不需要额外的激励就可以使大量员工签署协议。这样的话，在一

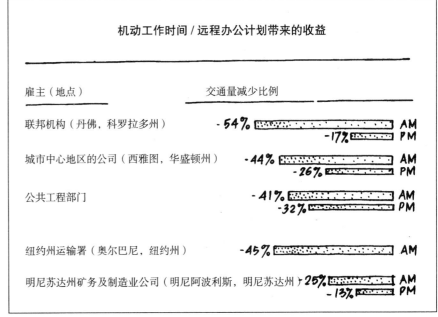

图片来源：R·尤图，TDM，发展管理和其他五分之一的交通，交通季刊，47卷，1993年。

些需要减少行程的社区，高峰时段的下降归于时间的调整而不是模式的转变[79]。向雇主提出他们的诉求，很难确定为何要修改工作时间，这在工作地区尤其寻常。

为非工作群体的 TDM

TDM 侧重于乘客，因为他们的行程集中在高峰时段并且每天都重复发生，但是随着工作出行只占日常出行的四分之一，并且只有大约一半的行程是在下午的高峰时段发生的，随着 TDM 申请受到限制，TDM 的效应也会受到限制。非工作目的出行管理包括（按照可能性由小到大的顺序）的选项包括：电脑"即时"拼车计划，邻里 TDM 计划，卡车送货 / 接人次数的限制，校车计划，先进的出行系统信息，提供避开交通堵塞区的出行路线，如果排除一些政治阻力，那么在交通拥堵时段向驾驶者收取过路费的计划就可能付诸实施[80]。

奥兰多的例子可以很好地诠释高科技手段在 TDM 中对非工作出行的管理，奥兰多的一个 TMA 劝说佛罗里达中心大学错开上课时间，同时，它为当地的运输公司签约校外公寓和大学之间的班车服务。没有任何技术的前提下，交通流量在早上高峰期下降了 31%，而日均访客人数则增长了 18%。

同样是在奥兰多，一项叫做 TravTek 的示范项目，可能是世界上最先进的关于车辆和驾驶员信息的技术系统，100 辆汽车（主要是租赁汽车）装备上了视频监控器、微型计算机、语音合成器和用于数据通信的无线电通信设备。由于和奥兰多车辆管理中心相连，机载系统可以提供最新的多样的交通信息，可以给驾驶者指明附近的餐馆、银行和其他服务设施，也可以给驾驶者提供可以选择的路线以缩短行程，一项测试表明驾驶时间可以被缩短 20%[81]。像 TravTek 这样先进的出行信息系统是组成智能交通系统的重要组成部分，而这个系统是 ISTEA 主动授权[82]和建立的。

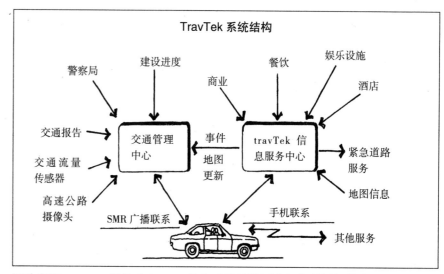

图片来源：J·H·里林《TravTek 信息时代的地面交通》美国智能车辆道路系统，华盛顿哥伦比亚特区，1992 年。

第六章　交通系统管理

当街道不能扩大，其通行能力可以通过优化道路交叉口来更有效地利用现有的街道宽度。

道格拉斯·哈伍德[83]

按照20世纪70年代的设想，交通体系管理（TSM）包括任何提高道路承载能力的手段，从实施拼车项目到进行交通设施的改善。

由于出行需求管理形成于自身，人们对于TSM的看法通常都局限于通过交通工程手段来提高道路的车辆容载率。TSM通常是对现有的交通网络做出改变而不是修建或者扩大新的设施。另外，TDM是影响驾驶者行为习惯的一门艺术[84]，而这也仅仅是TSM应用的冰山一角。

和TDM一样，TSM可以有效缓解居住密度过低带来的交通和行人过于稀少的问题，与TDM不同的是，TSM并不意味着在汽车使用上的任何约束，也许这就是为什么在佛罗里达州和其他的地方，与其他治理机动性的措施相比，TSM的应用更为广泛。

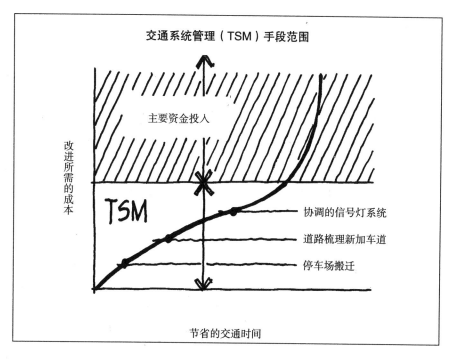

道路权利的再分配

在早期，TSM强调在道路自身范围内部的空间再分配，从而更好地适应交通高峰期出行，如今道路权利被重新分配：

划分行人路线以创造额外的（虽然窄）出行路线

删除隔离带以创建转弯车道或者额外的穿行道路

全天禁止路边停车或仅在高峰时段禁止

转换为单行道

创建方向可逆的单车道,早上和下午向不同的方向行驶

在适当的条件下,这些措施可以显著提高道路交通容量和平均行程速度[85]。每种措施都会付出一定的代价,比如高交通事故率、非高峰时段方向的速度变慢、路程长和街道的尺度不利于步行等。正是由于上述原因,下文中说的TSM措施才在今天得到了更多的关注。

可达性管理

从交通工程的角度看,道路扮演着两个迥然不同的角色:为房地产提供可达性和为交通工具提供可穿越性,在极端的情况下,高速公路不会给房地产提供直接可达性却可以提供大量的交通流,而尽头路却恰恰相反。

理论上讲,交通运行是干道的一个主要功能,也是支路的大部分功能。实际上,干道和支路都因为车道和出入口而变得杂乱无章,因而看起来更像地区性的道路。研究表明,随着出入口数量的增加,车辆运行速度会随之下降,同时事故率也会上升[86]。

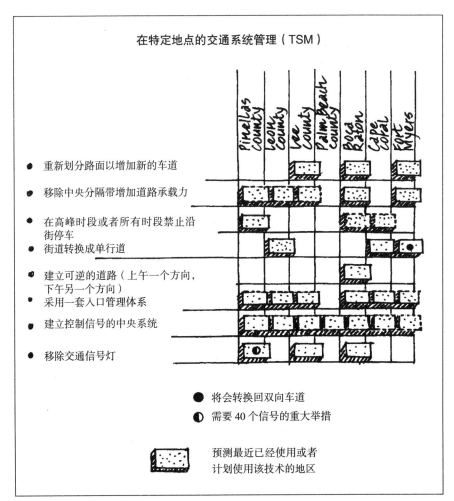

图片来源:作者在1995年中的调查研究。

为了应对这个趋势,综合交通管理部门采取一系列的措施——包括缩短车道间、交通信号灯间及地块出入口间的距离,在地块出入口的转弯处设置减速带,根据不同的道路类型和用地性质的要求,在过境交通的必要处设置转弯/加速/减速车道,以避开交通冲突点[87]。

在佛罗里达州有一个全国最雄心勃勃的可达性管理方案(与科罗拉多州,新泽西州,俄勒冈州一起),它控制着自己高速公路的出入口并在其辖区内推行可达性管理[88]。当地把土地划分成许多小块(每个地块都需要自己的车道),这些都严重地阻碍了可达性管理。为了帮助当地政府避免这种情况的发生,南佛罗里达大学城市交通研究中心(CUTR)制定了全州层面上更为细致的规定[89]。

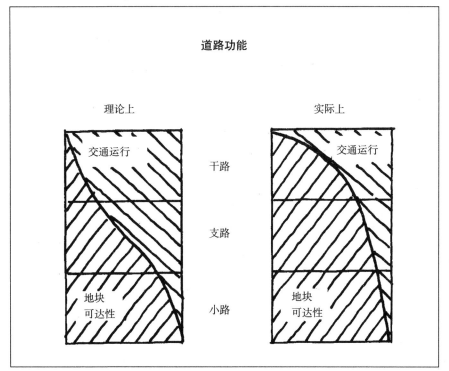

图片来源:R·尤因《居住区街道设计——有什么事儿英国人和澳大利亚人知道而我们美国人却不知道的》交通研究记录1945.5 交通研究委员会。华盛顿哥伦比亚特区。1994年。

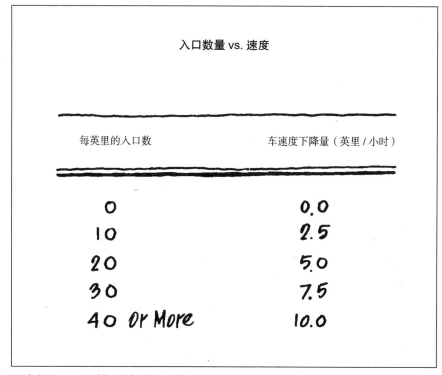

图片来源:D·爱斯玛特《入口管理-目前的先进技术》,第三届交通规划应用大会宣讲论文,交通研究委员会,华盛顿哥伦比亚特区,1991年。

道路交叉口的控制

干道和支路分别被各自的交叉口信号所控制，驾驶者从一个个路口奋力开动却只能等了又等。

在一个有众多交通信号和禁止左转的路网里，不考虑信号时间，在各个方向都取得良好的交通是不可能的。这一事实说明只有在简单的路口控制不起作用的时候交通信号才派得上用场，美国交通法规倾向于约束路口控制，交通信号被应用在回车处或者四车道的停车信号处，这样就可以保证安全并且减少等候时间[90]。双车道停车信号被安在让车标志处可以起到更好作用的地方[91]。

正如一个专家说的："英国的立体交通枢纽和道路交叉口的形式，交通控制的形式都是为了保护英国地面交通的顺畅以及尽可能地降低事故

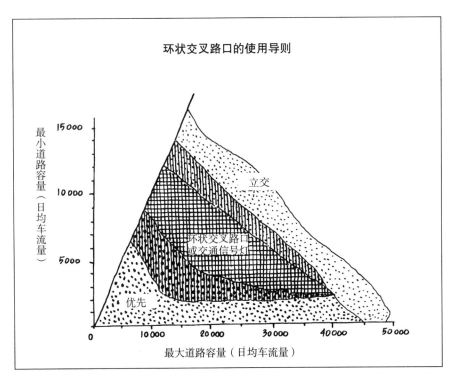

图片来源：公路交通运输机构，城市区域内的到来及交通，女王办公室，伦敦，1987年。

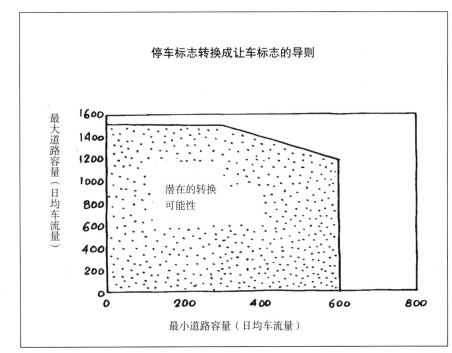

图片来源：H·W·麦吉和M·R·布兰肯西普，道路交叉口停车标志转换成让车标志的导则，国家合作交通运输研究项目报告，交通研究委员会，华盛顿哥伦比亚特区，1989年。

率,并牺牲少量的土地做道路用地。另一方面,美国偏爱的十字路口、停车标志、交通信号、宽阔的马路与狭窄的节点会导致很多不必要的延误、事故和土地、桥面、路面的浪费(着重加入)。"[92]

广泛应用于英国和澳大利亚的环形交叉口都是"宽节点"的极限,我们不是在谈论旧的、老式的交通圈而是不同原则("间隙"而不是"合并和编织")下的环形交叉路口的现代设计。环形交叉口交通允许车辆从不同的方向汇集在交叉路口,而交通信号则需要给予明确的交通指示。在流量比较均衡的时候这就显示了环形交叉口的容量优势[93]。正确设计的环形交叉口可以迫使车辆在进入路口的时候减速,然而在有绿灯、黄灯甚至是红灯的路口车辆却可以飞驰而过,这就使得环形交叉口有了安全上的优势[94]。环形交叉口也具备审美上的优势,它有一个中心岛景观可以打破宽阔路面所带来的视觉上的单调性,而且根据中心岛的大小,环形交叉口可能实施起来比交通信号等价格上更加低廉且耐用[95]。

这个想法看起来似乎很有吸引力。布雷登顿海滩、博卡拉顿、威尔、沃尔顿堡滩、那不勒斯、塔拉哈西、坦帕、塔瓦雷斯和西棕榈海滩最近都已经建立了环形交叉口。佛罗里达州的一些其他城市和乡村的环形交叉口也在设计和建设当中。佛罗里达交通部也制定了适用于全州的设计指导原则[96]。这使得佛罗里达州成为继加利福尼亚州和马里兰州之后第三个采用此方式的州[97],据澳大利亚和英国的消息人士透露,现在有很好的适合于那些想尝试"新"的形式和控制的地方政府和开发商的设计导则[98]。

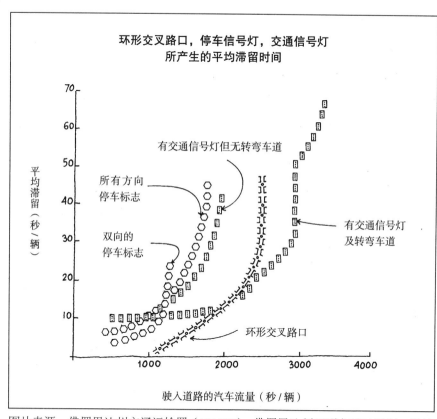

图片来源:佛罗里达州交通运输署(FDOT),佛罗里达州环形交叉口导则,塔拉哈西,1996年。数据假定交通总量中有20%的左转车辆,10%的右转车辆,60%的直行车辆。

在交通信号灯不可避免的地方,交通信号应该为车辆创造最短的停留[99]。从一开始,TSM就强调以更好的计时方法来协调交通信号,通过盖恩斯维尔、奥兰多、彭萨科拉和塔拉哈西的报道,通过以下一个或多个方面以使车辆在干道上的行程速度显著提高:给交通信号重新计时、转换为感应式交通信号、互相连接和协调的连续信号,并且在中央电脑下建立一个完整的网络系统[100]。佛罗里达州一直处于中央电脑控制领域的前列,在佛罗里达所有的大城市里,这样的设备都在运行之中。

先进的交通管理系统

由于高速公路智能系统提供"实时"的交通状况信息,在应对交通拥堵动态信息方面将来会做得更好。交通信号将会不断调整以优化交通流。高速公路的坡道将会被精心设计以优化交通主线上的交通流。高速

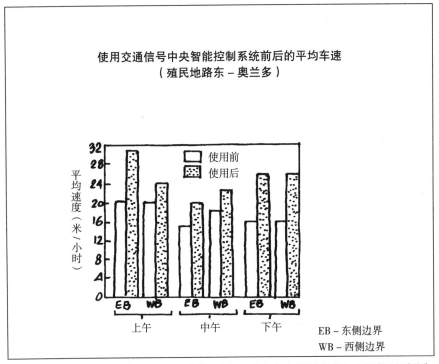

图片来源:F·R·阿雷曼及T·M·艾伦.《奥兰多大都市地区信息化交通信号系统》,ITE学术期刊使用第60卷,1990年6月。

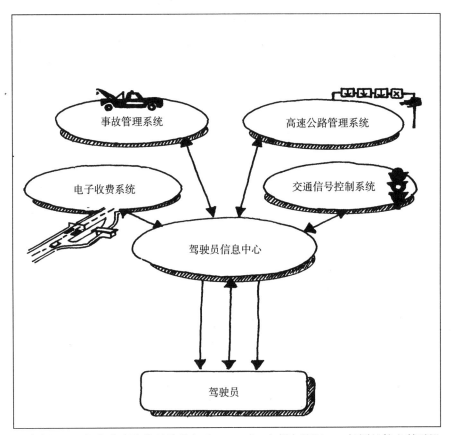

图片来源:联邦高速公路管理委员会(FHWA),大都市地区ITS部署的核心基础设施功能,华盛顿,1995年。

公路事故将被电子监测,事故车辆和其他隐患将被及时清除。最终,全国所有的245个最大的都市地区将有先进的交通管理系统,覆盖19000英里的高速公路和40000英里的干线公路[101]。先进的交通管理系统是构成智能交通运输系统的另一个"用户绑定服务"之一。迄今为止,潜在的出行延误将在10%~40%的范围之间[102]。

现在,佛罗里达几乎所有城市(也包括美国的其他地方)的交通信号系统都在白天工作,正常交通状况下一天中的不同时段计时计划会被相应地激活。条件出现异常时,这些系统就不会做出反应,在这一方面美国滞后于一些其他兄弟国家[103]。

我们期望看到交通朝着交通响应和交通自适应的方向发展,克里尔沃特、圣彼得堡和品艾拉斯都已经有交通响应系统,这个系统可以在一些有争议的交叉路口监视车辆并且为他们制定最合适的计时策略。哈利法克斯、新斯科舍、奥克斯纳德、加利福尼亚、多伦多和安大略都已经建成了英国最完整的交通自适应系统。SCOOL、阿灵顿县、弗吉尼亚州、丘拉维斯塔、加利福尼亚、明尼阿波利斯以及明尼苏达也正在做着同样的事情。奥克兰县、密歇根县、新城堡、特拉华、和郊区亨内平县和明尼苏达是最早一批建立澳大利亚完整交通自适应系统SCATS的地方。

针对美国的需求,联邦高速公路管理处开发RT-TRACS系统。交通自适应系统随着流量的波动不断调整和优化信号设置,在交通堵塞发生前对其作出预测[104]。他们可以在拥堵杂乱的交通状况下缩短10%、20%甚至30%的出行时间[105]。佛罗里达州的ISO部门第一次测试这项技术。在Ft.代尔堡,它使得一条干道的通行时间降低了15%~20%。有了这一成功先例,佛罗里达州运输部要在贯穿全县的拥挤道路上安装SCATS,并证明SCATS可以在全州范围内使用。

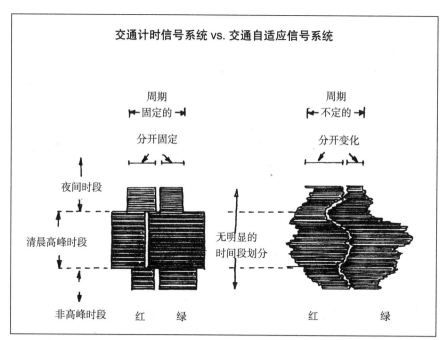

图片来源:引自P·T·马丁及S·L·M·霍克蒂《快速更新》交通计时信号系统。

高速公路延误有将近三分之二是由交通事故和其他事件引起的[106]，即所说的"非经常性事件"，类似这样的延误似乎每天都会发生，因为有车道被封闭，车辆通行数目下降。为了更快的应对这种状况，在城市的高速公路上都装备有完善的事故管理系统，包括交通检测器、监控摄像机、电子资讯和事件管理团队。

通过与地面交通相协调的运营管理，全国的交通更向前迈进了一步[107]。沿着迈阿密和棕榈滩县之间的95号州际公路将城市走廊作为一个整体管理，佛罗里达东南部的智能走廊项目将运用探测器和监视相机进行检测和监控路面事件；用电子资讯设备和电子资讯广播来重新给路面车辆制定路线。县域的中央电脑会重新计算以给更多的车辆制定绕行路线，交通仪器（交通信号可以控制进入区域内车辆比例）将会在迈阿密I-95号公路上所有的入口处安装。佛罗里达外围的高速控制仪已经在减少事故、增加车流量、增加干道速度方面展现出了惊人的效果[108]，在未来的某一天，迈阿密的控制仪和交通信号可以共同为减少拥堵做出贡献[109]。

在 ISTEA 精神指引下（毕竟其中有联合运输的含义），佛罗里达东南部智能走廊也将自动定位车辆位置并获得出行人信息。使用停车换乘设施的司机会确切地知道下一班汽车或者火车什么时间到达。那些进入或离开机场或港口地区的车辆将可以即时获得路况信息（也有高速的）。我们的目标是无缝的交通连接。

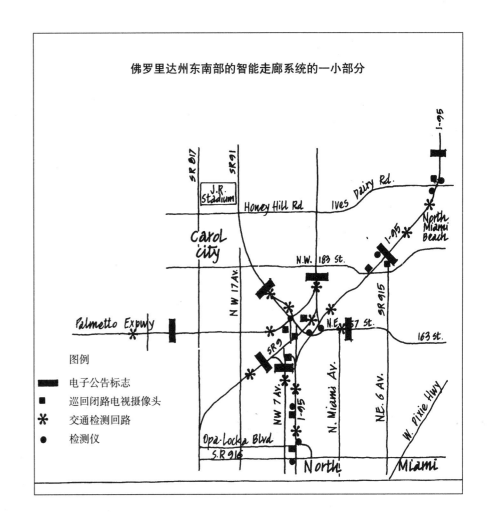

第七章 增强运输服务

……政策制定者应对分散化形成的挑战所制定的对策:(1)使运输服务更加灵活……(2)调整土地的使用功能使其更支持运输……

罗伯特切尔韦罗[110]

加拿大和澳大利亚的城市人口总密度和汽车所有权与美国类似,但他们有三倍或三倍以上的交通客流量。这些城市已经成功地创造出有利于交通运输的条件[111]。

美国的一些城市也已经开始做同样的事情[112]。也许佛罗里达州最好的例子是奥兰多,那里的交通运营商正在寻求一个愿景:"在提供和协调全方位运输服务方面成为公认的世界级领导者。"自1990年以来它一直处在美国客流量增长最快的城市阵营中。奥兰多的经验表明即使在佛罗里达州,这个有汽车依赖的城市典型,运输仍然可以有所进展。

佛罗里达州所选定城市的交通运输特性方面的创新

	佛罗里达劳德代尔堡	盖恩斯维尔	杰克逊维尔	迈阿密	奥兰多	塔拉哈西	坦帕
以交通为导向的设计手册	—	—	—	—	2	—	1
有自行车架的公共汽车/公共汽车总量	1/196	10/55	0/165	2P/598	3/185（大学城环线）	7/64	170/170
定时的换乘中心	10 部分协调	市中心	—	20（部分调整）	6+ 市中心	市中心	4+ 市中心
拼车	—	—	—	—	60	—	25P（取代两个固定路线）
兼职司机/全职司机	5/408	0/62	0/273	104/1,146	6/320	20/79 菲联堡	12/247
已签约的固定路线	9（接驳巴士路线）	—	—	8（换线/接驳巴士路线）	2P（快线）	—	2/2P（环线/接驳巴士路线）

资料来源:1995年年中作者的调查。

交通运输走廊和节点

在北美，目前大约有 50 种关于以公共交通为导向的开发（TOD）手册得到应用，未来会更多[113]。奥兰多和坦帕的交通运营商已经准备了当地的使用手册，而佛罗里达州运输部也制定了在全州范围内使用的手册[114]。

其中一个最有名的以公交为导向的开发模式（TOD）手册倡导发展交通走廊，另一个更有名的手册倡导发展交通节点[115]。无论采取哪种方法，手册一致认为成功取决于中高密度的中转站布点，满足每四分之一英里设置一个中转站点。而被广泛接受的可满足基本公共汽车服务的最小密度，是居住用地每英亩设置七个中转站点[116]。

我们研究了迈阿密的交通客流量，表明：中转站布点密度要两倍于最小密度以便维持系统的平均生产率[117]。在美国以公共交通为导向的开发正在向更高的密度发展，通常为每英亩 20 到 30 个中转站点[118]。

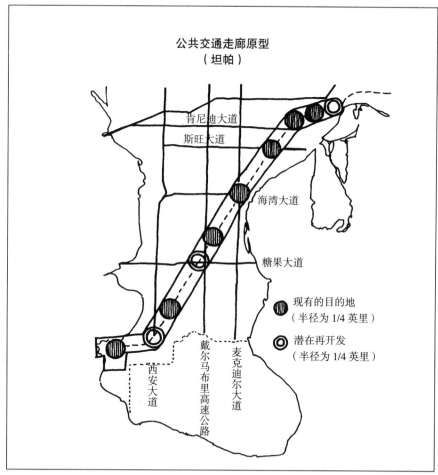

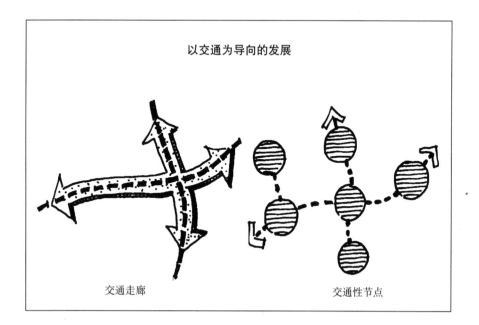

资料来源：林克斯及其合伙人公司，交通友好型开发，希尔斯堡地区区域交通管理局，佛罗里达州坦帕市，1994 年。

手册还赞成在中转站点周围混合布置住宅和商业用地。土地的混合使用可以为过境用户提供一个24小时都生机勃勃的环境，并允许他们如汽车用户一样上下班[119]。

土地使用被以交通兼容性标准进行评分[120]。学校、公寓和办公楼得到了很高的评分，汽车旅馆、折扣店和仓库得分较低。这样做是为了引导兼容性好的用地发展为交通走廊或节点，并将不兼容的以汽车为导向的用地腾出来。

土地规划和法规已经被修订来鼓励在亚特兰大、波特兰、圣地亚哥和许多其他地方的TOD模式。市场也作出了回应[121]。南迈阿密是佛罗里达州第一个作出回应的城市，它改写了开发代码来促进地铁站点周围以公共交通为导向的开发。新的设计标准已被采用，并给地下停车场、公共广场、人行拱廊和混合三个或更多土地用途的项目提供开发激励政策。

佛罗里达州的第一个关于郊区的TOD模式的提出是针对于一条通勤铁路线的建设，其具体位置是在坦帕市外的威斯特查斯的主计划社区的

交通运输兼容性图表			
	机动交通	本地交通	高兼容性交通
商业			
酒店	◐	◐	◐
汽车旅馆	◉	◉	◉
电影院	◉	◉	◉
餐馆	◐	◐	◐
购物中心			
邻里单位	◉	◉	◉
社区	◉	◉	◉
区域	◉	◉	◉
免下车和穿过式商业	◉		
折扣店			
百货商店	◐	◐	◐
便利店	◉	◉	◐
◉ 大多数兼容			
◐ 有时兼容			

资料来源：引自斯诺克米西县交通运输管理局，土地利用和交通运输导则，技术共享计划，美国交通运输署，华盛顿哥伦比亚特区，1989年。

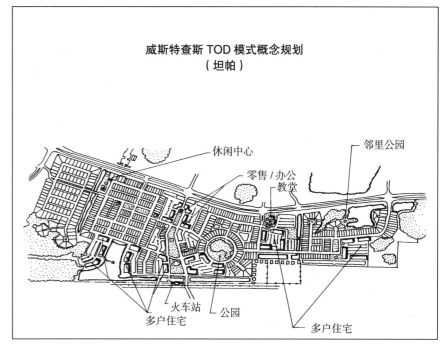

资料来源：美国土地开发公司，佛罗里达州坦帕市。

一小部分。在早期的概念性规划中，TOD提出建设一个多用途的城镇中心的计划，包含地面上的公寓和地下的商店，周围环绕着的办公室、公寓和小批量单户住房。要想建立中转车站和一个居民拥有汽车替代方案的社区，开发商可以拥有更高的建设密度并且可以不完全满足道路服务水平的标准（依据1993年佛罗里达州开发管理法律——见第二章）。

扩展服务领域

研究告诉我们，人们骑自行车几英里后需要一个中转站点暂时停留。这是典型的步行距离的8倍，意味着骑自行车者可达的服务面积是步行者的64倍。运输车辆上的自行车拖架的安装不仅可以使自行车用于运输而且可以成为旅程终点的出站口；它还是汽车模式（停泊及转乘模式）不能匹敌的容易进出的模式。与汽车的停泊及转乘站点相比，自行车停车处很廉价；一辆汽车停车的空间可以存储10辆自行车[122]。

加利福尼亚州圣巴巴拉通过设置较为廉价的自行车停车和公共汽车后面的自行车拖车的措施增加了46%的交通客流量[123]。迈阿密的地铁–戴德交通系统中有半数的火车站拥有自行车存放柜，并允许自行车在非高峰时段进入火车厢体内停车。佛罗里达州一些城市的公交运营商使用经过试验测试的自行车架并在一些运输中心安装上了自行车车架。迄今

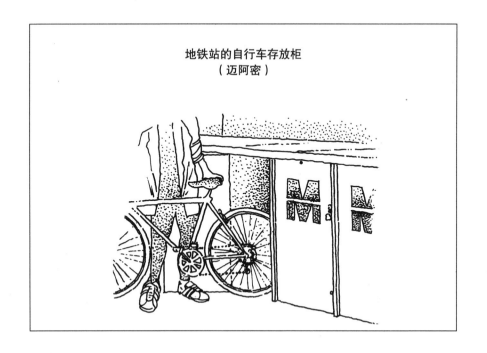

地铁站的自行车存放柜
（迈阿密）

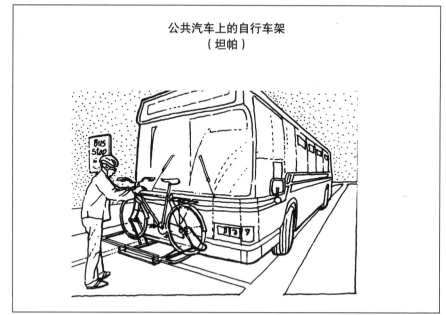

公共汽车上的自行车架
（坦帕）

为止坦帕的计划是最雄心勃勃的,所有车队中的公共汽车都必须安装自行车车架,每月的使用量已经从最初的 250 个开始上升,预计一年后达到 2500 个,两年后达到 4000 个。

早期来自坦帕和其他城市的结果说明了一个明显的结论:在长途的、区域的旅行中,自行车的中转环节是最有用的设置。在盖恩斯维尔和塔拉哈西等小城市以及奥兰多的佛罗里达州中部大学的那些穿梭路线中,骑自行车是所有到达目的地的方式中最快、最经济的。

那些机动车驾驶员大约平均 5 英里需要停泊及转乘站点。这是典型步行需要停息站点距离的 20 倍,意味着驾驶员的服务面积是行人的 400 倍。如果某些条件得到满足,停泊及转乘站点可以设置在郊区。基本上,停泊及转乘需要中等的居住密度、一个良好的交通走廊、一个通到市中心的长途公交站或通过快速公交连接的就业中心(据估计 15~50 英里)[124]。交通走廊的专用拼车车道的可用性可以提高停泊及转乘站点间隔,同时停泊及转乘站点的可用性也可以提高专用拼车车道的使用效率[125]。停泊及转乘站点的安全措施和设施也可以发挥作用[126]。

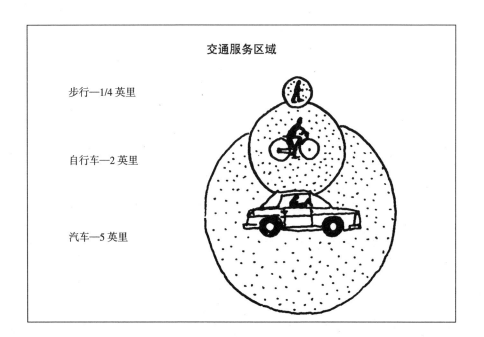

停车换乘站点所需的要素的重要性排名
(由高到低)

#1	安全
#2	照明
#3	公交服务
#4	付费电话
#5	避风雨的等待区
#6	垃圾桶
#7	公交/拼车信息
#8	景观
#9	自动售货机
#10	自行车车架
#11	日托机构

资料来源:W·E·赫里尔、A·A·斯格拉基斯和 S·B·科勒曼"配合停车换乘与 HOV 设施规划的选址及需求预测模型的应用"交通工程师协会(ITE)1994 年科技论文汇编,交通工程师协会,华盛顿哥伦比亚特区,1994 年。

虽然佛罗里达州有很多停泊及转乘站点（据统计至少有 99 个）。大多数几乎不能提供安全装置或设施，有些只提供少得可怜的服务，许多站点没有得到有效维护。很少有站点同时满足所有上述三个标准，因此它的使用率很低。国家采取不同的政策，现在正在兴建很多停泊及转乘站点[127]。这些站点都是与佛罗里达州东南部 I-95 公路上的通勤铁路车站相伴的。用户可以选择在一个更安全、舒适的等候环境下选择停车换乘铁路、公共汽车或选择在州际专用拼车车道行驶的专用拼车。

减少交通运行时间

交通用户讨厌从一个公共汽车换乘到另一个公共汽车。排除任何等待时间，换乘本身含有的"负效用"等同于 30 分钟的骑自行车的时间[128]。因此，只要有可能，路程安排应该尽量避免换乘，即便需要额外的骑自行车的时间。

如今，在多核心的大都市地区换乘是不可避免的[129]。在交通服务不频繁的情况下，大多数地方大多数时间，通过定时换乘可以保证所用时间最少且服务可靠性最大[130]。很多公交线路大约同时汇聚到同一个换乘中心，就像航空公司的航班汇聚到一个枢纽机场一样。在很多城市，定时换乘扭转了交通客流量下降的趋势[131]。经过证实，它可以有效地降低在中等密度城市（如密歇根州安阿伯市和俄勒冈州波特兰市）短途旅行的时间[132]。坦帕在五个区域商场设有定时换乘站点，奥

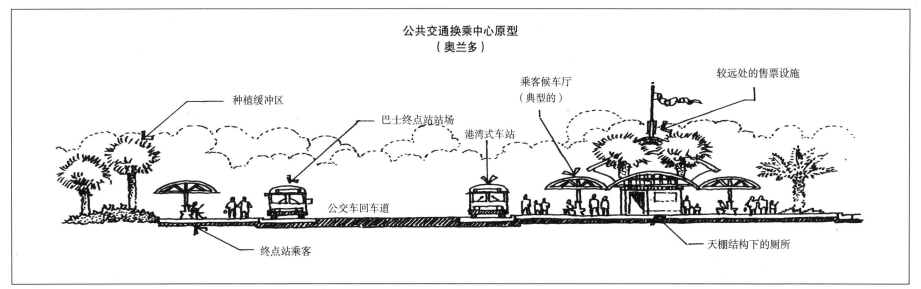

资料来源：赫伯特－哈尔巴克公司，Lynx-客户设施手册，佛罗里达州中部地区交通管理局，奥兰多，1994 年。

兰多在三个商场、佛罗里达州中部大学、奥兰多国际机场、一个邻里中心以及市中心设有定时换乘站点。奥兰多和坦帕市计划在主要传输点建设高舒适性中转中心。

即使没有转车，运输也有汽车的一个固有劣势，它需要走路和等待。运输站点可以通过给交通干道添加支路而得到贯通。许多国家大城市有市区公交车道，少数大城市有连接市中心的拼车主干公路[133]。公共汽车 / 专用拼车车道利用塑料贴、路钉或其他类似的东西明显区别开一般车道，增强其有效性；在路口，公交车通过抢占、相位修正或队列跳转等信号享有优先通过权，同时积极实施 HOV 的限制[134]。从一些源头来讲，公共汽车 / 专用拼车车道指南和其他车道优先措施是有效的[135]。

迈阿密南迪克西公路，这条南部最重要的交通动脉，在公共汽车 / 拼车车道方面是一个成功的先例[136]。它在 1997 年初开通了一条与南迪克西公路平行的公共汽车专用公路，减少了在这条九英里走廊运行的十分钟公共汽车时间。通过交通信号改变使定时的直达公交和即将到来的公交优先通过十字路口[137]。这个交通系统使用户在停车换乘地铁车站到迈阿密市区这段距离不需要停车。通过在车站内部设置上 / 下车站点提供免费的换乘以及调度频繁的公共汽车、铁路服务，使"转乘处罚"一直保持到绝对最小值。

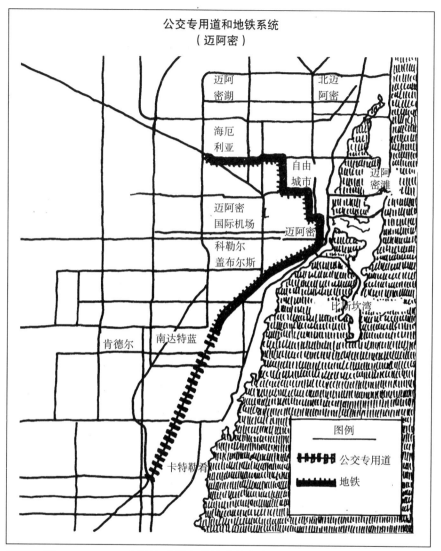

资料来源：B.C. Fowler "乔治亚州南戴德公交车专用道"交通工程师学会（ITE）1995 年科技论文汇编，交通工程师协会，华盛顿哥伦比亚特区，1995 年。@1995 年交通工程师协会授权使用。

奥兰多市中心计划的公交车道建设，将使公交车往来市中心的速度比汽车还快。车道一般与常规车道分开，增加中线、岛或半球形的分隔符（"按钮"）。交通信号会被即将到来的公共汽车的信号激活，变绿灯早一点或保持绿灯多亮一会儿，以便更好地服务。

许多大城市也有高速拼车车道，可以有效地排除自驾车的情况[138]。这些都不像佛罗里达州东南部的I-95公路或奥兰多的I-4公路那种钻石级车道，而是物理上分开的车道。同时这种物理分隔的公路也比较容易进行执法。在被间隔分开的车道上自驾车犯罪率很少超过10%，然而在正常车道上很少低于10%[139]。

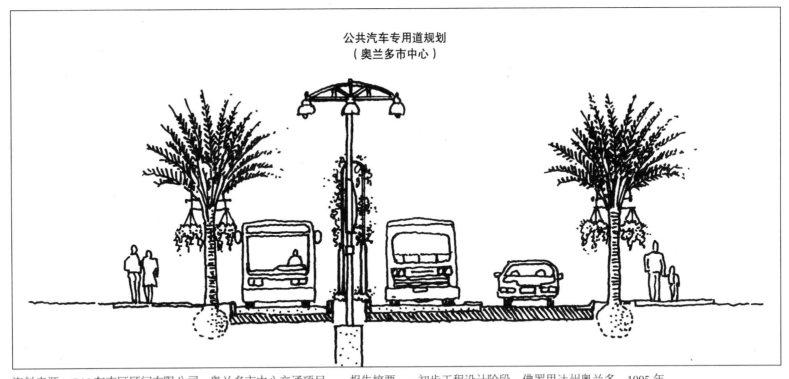

资料来源：GAI东南区顾问有限公司，奥兰多市中心交通项目——报告摘要——初步工程设计阶段，佛罗里达州奥兰多，1995年。

专用拼车车道可以使长途旅行节省多达 30 分钟时间，这个数据也取决于一般车道的拥挤程度。节省时间越多，就会有更多独行上班族选择共同出行[140]。据估计，当旅行节约时间超过 0.8 分钟 / 英里，或者总共达到 8 分钟的时候，专用拼车车道比较有效[141]。

公众对专用拼车车道最满意的地方在于这种车道属于当地大的拼车体系的一部分[142]。例如，明尼阿波利斯的集成公路系统，由该国的第一个专用拼车车道、高速公路支路坡道（相对于测量的通用坡道）、三个与州际公路直接连接的市中心停车泊位和低利用率的拼车、很多运输和拼车用户使用的七个由沿着州际的停泊及转乘站点、多用途直达城市的公交服务和定时换乘的公交服务组成[143]。这里还有为旅行者提供的先进信息服务，旅行者可以从放置在住宅、办公场所、购物中心和中转站的终端掌握"实时"交通安排和交通信息[144]。

按照佛罗里达州的 1991 州际公路政策，一般使用的车道数量仅限于 6 个；任何附加车道（共为 10 个）必须是通过障碍分隔开的专用拼车车道。而根据 1996 年的政策，仍比较偏向在可以承受的条件下建设拼车车道。专用拼车车道将在杰克逊维尔、坦帕和奥兰多的州际高速公路上进行建设。

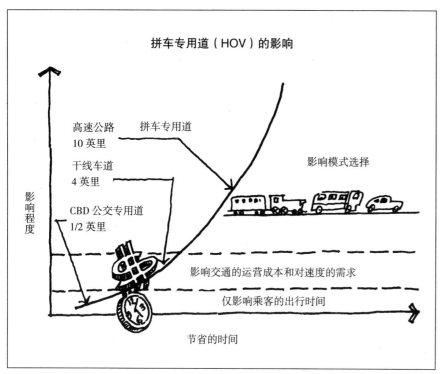

资料来源：引自 H·S·莱文森"干路上的拼车专用道"正在进行的第二届全国拼车专用道及交通方式会议，技术共享办公室，美国交通运输署，华盛顿哥伦比亚特区，1987 年。

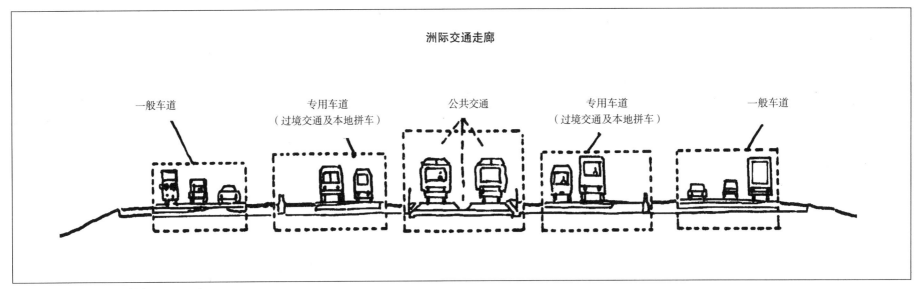

资料来源：佛罗里达运输部（FDOT）。

非传统服务

郊区的人口密度往往过低以至于不能支持常规公共汽车服务，这一点在非高峰期更加明显。即便如此，公共交通模式也不能取消。在杂乱无章的城市，工作场所远离住宅的情况下，拼车可以代替固定常规的路线服务；合同出租车服务则在周末或晚上代替固定常规的路线服务[145]。至少54个运营商在全国范围内提供响应需求的没有固定路线的服务；11个运营商提供常规时间以外的服务[146]。

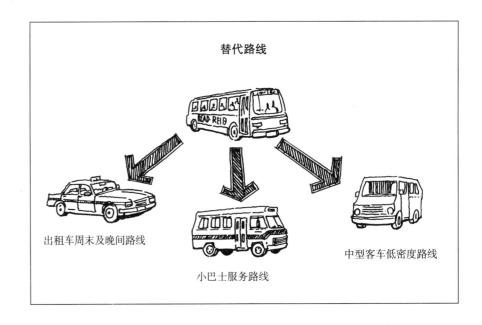

十年前，布里瓦德放弃了常用的公交车路线，开通了通往肯尼迪航天中心的拼车上班服务和为老年人和残疾人设立的拨号叫车服务。虽然有些常规线路已经得到恢复，拼车上班的人仍然占了高峰时的交通人数、服务时间和总乘客英里的最大份额（大约 100 万／月）。布里瓦德的交通运营商以及那些在清水、圣彼得堡、湖畔和奥兰多的运营商，用联邦交通援助购买了货车，然后反过来以低于市场利率的价格租借给下面的客户（只有维护、保险和行政成本）。这样的安排会削减一半以上的月租。

同样，在服务路线上的面包车有时可以代替班车服务（或在某种情况下的拨号叫车服务）。在欧洲流行的一种情况是，服务路线穿过社区进入停车场，车开到建筑入口并采取停车开车（随叫随停）或路线偏差（短途绕远）的模式[147]。在短途路线情况下，面包车在一般的上座率和峰值需求的情况下表现出了经济性[148]。

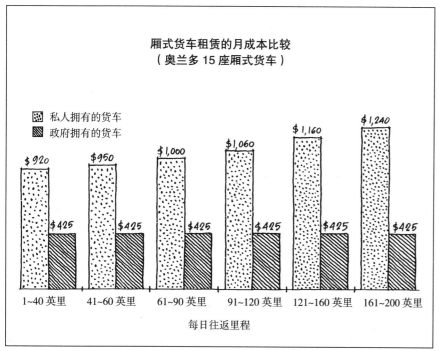

资料来源：VPSI 公司，奥兰多，佛罗里达。

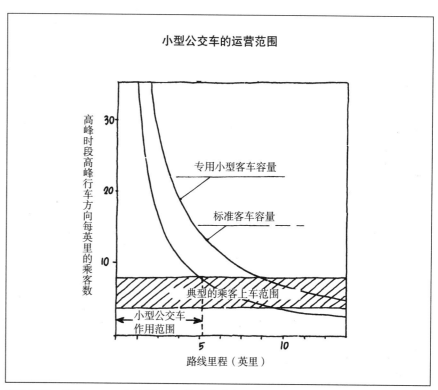

资料来源：引自 S·J·安德烈、F·斯皮尔伯格和 A·汉格布勒，小型公交车的运营成本及特征，城市轨道交通管理委员会，美国交通运输署，华盛顿哥伦比亚特区，1981 年。

布劳沃德执行社区公交路线计划，为八个小城市提供了面包车服务[149]。奥兰多在不能通行长途大巴的老地区使用面包车提供服务；戴德也使用面包车提供从边远郊区到地铁站的支线服务。

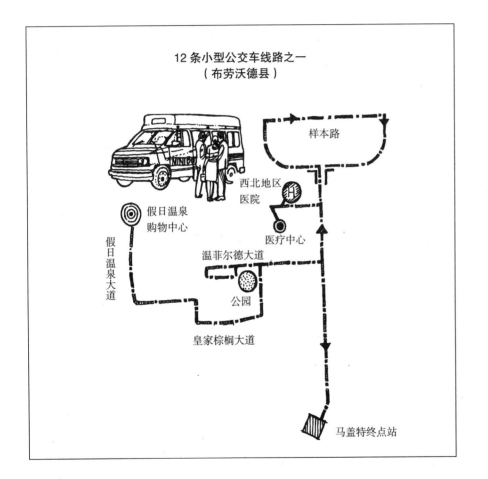

操作经济体

交通运营商抱怨采用双重标准对待他们[150]。对汽车的大力补贴，似乎没有人介意（见在第一章的讨论）。然而，交通补贴则引起了政客和民众的愤怒。

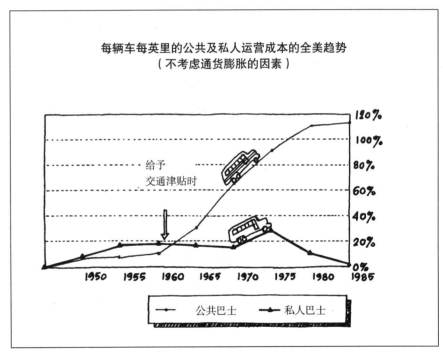

资料来源：J·拉沃和W·考克斯，交通服务的竞争性合同，智慧基金会，洛杉矶，加利福尼亚州，1993年。经智慧基金会HTG5许可转载，@1993年"智慧基金会"授权使用。

这种抱怨虽然是正当的却也无关紧要（政治上来说），因为汽车补贴是被巧妙地隐藏起来了，而运输补贴则是对大众透明的。从20世纪七十年代至今，在运输过程中，运营成本和补贴需求出现了无情的上升趋势。运输的长期生存能力必须确保对这个趋势的压制行之有效。

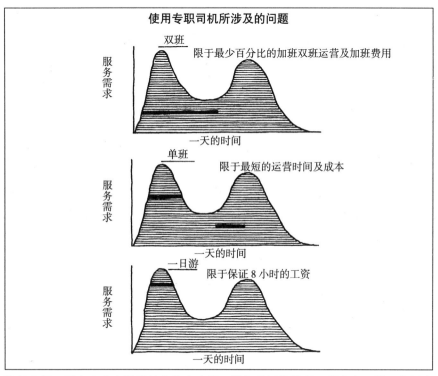

资料来源：引自麦克多曼及其合伙人公司，附加的运营管理：程序和工具，交通实践集9，交通运输研究委员会，华盛顿哥伦比亚特区，1985年。

几乎所有的美国大型交通系统都建立了工会组织。这导致工人拥有相对于私人公司在相应的岗位更高的工资和以任何标准而言都更为丰厚的附加福利（平均55%的工资和薪金）[151]。这也导致难以实施高效利用劳动力的工作规则[152]。在大的城市地区，交通需求量的高峰出现在早上和下午，大约三分之二的日常交通旅客在这两个高峰期乘车[153]。按照严格限制的工作规则，被雇来满足高峰需求的司机并不能有效地在其他时间发挥作用[154]。

虽然在某种情况下公司可以为全职司机制定免于从事过长时间工作并补偿他们长期等待高峰间隔的工作规则，但是为兼职司机制定公平的工作规则就较为困难了。兼职司机可以用来填充高峰时期的空缺，而这些空缺对于全职司机而言就是需要溢价费用或加班费。全职司机将失去一些他们习惯了的额外补偿。但也将获得一些好处，那就是像一般工人一样的工作时间。

兼职司机的使用可以降低3%~8%的司机赔偿总成本（或更多），准确的百分比取决于传播规则的限制程度和早上、下午两个高峰的人流密度[155]。兼职司机在事故率、员工流动率、缺勤率方面像全职司机一样表现出色，这代表着为交通运营商争取到更多净收益[156]。

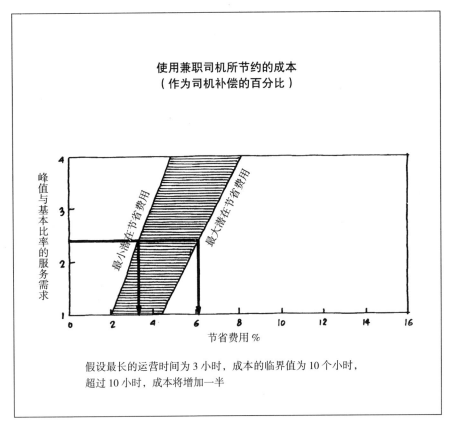

资料来源：麦克多曼及其合伙人公司，兼职运营商的应用，交通实践集9，交通运输研究委员会，华盛顿哥伦比亚特区，1986年。

运输服务可以承包给私人运营商来得到更大的利润。在里根执政期间，联邦政府推行的运输外包或私有化进程的策略产生了比任何其他联邦交通政策都更大的争议[157]。支持承包的条文是："已知的信息令人信服地说明，竞争服务承包可以得到大量长期或短期的成本和补贴储蓄。"[158] 在私人承包商取代了公共交通部门并提供相同或非常类似的服务的情况下，公司节约的成本大约在二到四成[159]。此外，这些储蓄在逐渐减少，因为投标价格在真正的条款中普遍下降（通胀调整后），而公共交通运营成本不断上升。

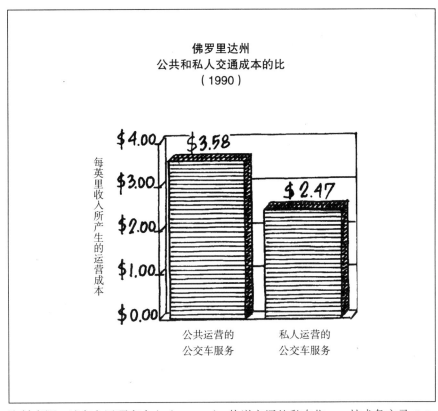

资料来源：城市交通研究中心（CUTR），轨道交通的私有化——技术备忘录#2，南佛罗里达大学，坦帕，1993年。

公平地说，通过合同外包节约成本有时会以牺牲服务质量和上座率为代价。戴德、棕榈滩、丹佛、新奥尔良和佛罗里达州外其他一些地方，不得不终止服务合同，原因在于很多车辆晚点、错过车次、求助电话和用户投诉。

公共交通部门必须在招标签订合同过程中投入很大的精力。可从几个来源得到竞争承包的指导原则[160]。它最好能是逐渐地、部分地从公有向私有过渡[161]。通过"涟漪效应"，承包的常见威胁似乎唤起了公共交通运营商和其工会实行成本削减措施[162]。同样，内部操作的延续可帮助保持年度招标过程的竞争力[163]。

全州总购买收入英里数，包括需求和快速响应服务，总收入从1984年的2%上升到1990年的15%[164]。四个交通系统承租常规公交车服务，一个承租连接三轨铁路的支线公交服务，一个承租直达公交服务。外包运营可以使每英里的成本平均削减大约三分之一。

	公共交通服务的 竞争性合同原则
公共控制	☑ 服务设计 ☑ 服务监督 ☑ 与负责人的基础价最低的投标人签定合同
竞争市场	☑ 对于所有潜在投标者进行竞标 ☑ 招标书明确规定的服务要求 ☑ 可为服务的小部分增加而订立合同 ☑ 合同和续约总共不超过五年 ☑ 合同到期续约时间彼此不同（多个合同） ☑ 有限的市场份额 ☑ 定价合同 ☑ 公共机构组织的公平参与
完全开放的过程	☑ 开放的前期会议 ☑ 积极宣传招标工作 ☑ 所有利益相关方的招标书和合同副本

资料来源：J·拉沃和W·考克斯，交通服务的竞争性合同，智慧基金会，洛杉矶，加利福尼亚州，1993年。经智慧基金会HTG5许可转载。@1993年"智慧基金会"。

第八章　有利于行人和骑自行车人的设计

在汽车的海洋里，行人只有行走在小而独立的安全岛上才会感到舒服。比如公园、大学校园、购物中心和新公寓。但是这些地方却总是脱离了有真正活动的街道。

理查德·尤特曼（Richard Untermann）[165]

为了娱乐目的出行时 90% 的美国人选择步行方式，至少一半的人偶尔骑自行车出行，90% 住在市中心的人都是步行，购物者在封闭式购物中心行走几英里是十分常见的。根据 1990 年美国人口普查，在 100 个中型城市和乡镇工作的通勤人员中，超过 15% 的人选择步行或骑自行车的方式去上班[166]。

因此美国人会在合适的条件下选择步行或骑自行车。问题是，在佛罗里达的大部分地区没有"合适"条件存在。在全美的步行或自行车城市调查中，只有一个佛罗里达州的城市基韦斯特排名在前 100。

良好的意愿

作为全美骑自行车和步行研究的一部分，规划和设计导则在各个州和地方之间进行比较的结论是："目前，佛罗里达州提供了全美范围内最全面的自行车和步行设施设计方法……"[167]

部分美国城市和城镇的步行／骑自行车上班的比例
（1990）

	排名	步行／骑自行车比例
普林斯顿，纽约州	#1	54%
米林顿，田纳西州	#6	47%
牛津，俄亥俄州	#10	38%
戴维斯，加利福尼亚州	#21	27%
艾奥瓦城，艾奥瓦州	#33	23%
基韦斯特，佛罗里达州	#49	21%
哥伦比亚，南卡罗来纳州	#64	19%
博尔德，科罗拉多州	#67	19%
普洛佛，犹他州	#87	16%
波士顿，马萨诸塞州	#99	15%
盖恩斯维尔，佛罗里达州	#104	14%

资料来源：特定表格，1990 年美国人口及住房普查，电子文件汇编 3 A。

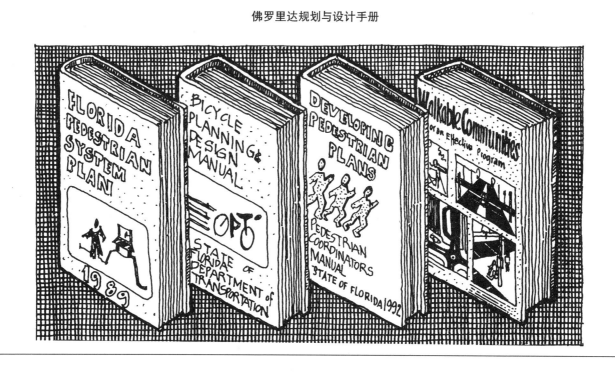

佛罗里达规划与设计手册

如果我们幸运地工作在佛罗里达州,为什么步行和骑自行车的这么少呢?原因之一在于,步行和骑自行车的数量很大程度上源于步行和自行车设施的发展模式,而佛罗里达州的发展模式并不尽如人意,不仅如此,(直到最近)佛罗里达州的行人和自行车设施甚至差到难以用语言来形容。

让旅途简短

步行和骑自行车的速度比汽车慢了很多,而且在出行过程中没有任何像汽车一样的温度调节设备、娱乐设备和金属外壳保护,这使得他们更加在乎出行中的路程长度和环境。

在短途出行中步行和骑自行车是可以取代在同里程的基础上更污染和耗油的汽车的。步行对于几乎所有长度小于 0.1 英里的出行都是最合适的选择;但当里程达到 1.5 英里以上时人们只有 10% 的可能会选择步行[168]。考虑到自行车的速度更快,出行距离可以更长,但是以工作、购物等为目的的自行车出行仍然通常不到 2 英里[169]。

通过混合土地使用和集群发展（见第四章）可以缩短出行距离从而鼓励步行或骑自行车。在涉及了近4000位成年人的调查中显示，紧凑发展在增加步行和骑自行车比率的措施之中排第一位。保证购物和办理其他个人业务的位置在家的半英里范围内，工作地点在两英里范围内，以及独立使用的人行道和自行车道或每加仑上涨2美元的汽油价格等因素使步行和骑自行车的数量转变为汽车出行的两倍[170]。

出行距离也可以通过良好的场地规划来缩短。步行的人，特别是喜欢遵循最短路径、最少转弯的人，都尽可能地使他们的路线保持直线。短而直的街道、捷径和建筑旁边或背后的停车位这种小空间，都能使距离最小化。

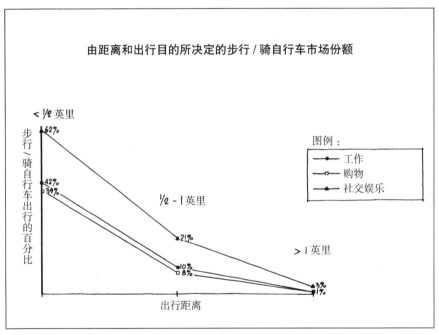

图片来源：特定表格，1990年，全国范围的个人交通调查（NPTS）。

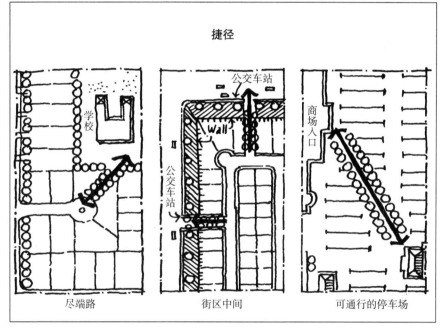

图片来源：引自 R.K. Untermann，"市郊地区的社区改造"，《迎合行人——适宜步行和自行车交通的城镇及邻里单位》，范·诺丝丹·莱因霍尔德有限公司，纽约，1984年；斯诺荷密什郡交通管理局，土地利用及公共交通导则。技术共享计划，美国交通运输部，华盛顿，1989年；W·鲍斯，M·格莱沃和G·诺克森，深化设计及审批过程中交通因素的注意事项，加拿大安大略省渥太华市，1991年。

让旅行安全

1995年,佛罗里达的自行车出行死亡率占全国首位,是全国平均水平的三倍。步行的人死亡率高达第四位,几乎是全国平均水平的两倍。这确实使佛罗里达人把步行和骑自行车看成是危险的,从而导致他们不采用这些出行方式。

这些因素并不足以为步行和骑自行车的人创建像绿洲一样独立的交通通道。但我们必须开始为他们提供像汽车公路网络一样的连续网络通道。保证除了低密度住宅区之外所有的街道都遍布了人行道。

增加安全区和避难群岛为行人在横跨宽阔街道的途中提供了避风港。人行横道在过大的街区中为一些横穿街道的行人提供了保护,再配备上单独的行人信号灯,就能让人行横道提供更多的保护。十字路口良好的照明能使行人在晚上的视野更清晰。通道控制并限制了车道和中央隔离岛的数量,从而限制了潜在冲突点的数量,这些措施的成效是有据可查的[171]。

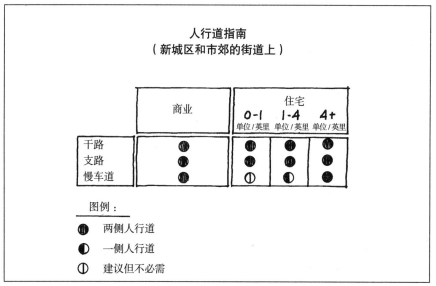

图片来源:引自R·L·克诺伯劳等人。《基于行人交通事故多发区域的调查:人行横道,人行道,当地街道及主要干道》,联邦高速公路管理局,华盛顿哥伦比亚特区,1988年。

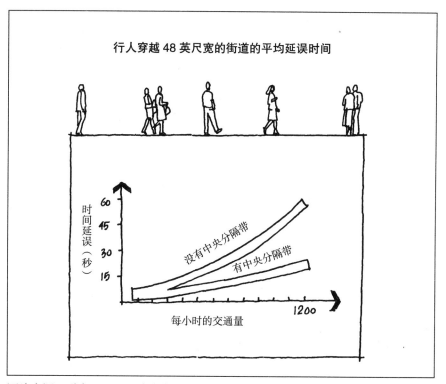

图片来源:引自:S·A·史密斯,市郊及开发中的乡村地区的步行设施的规划及实施,国家合作高速公路研究项目报告294A,交通研究委员会,华盛顿哥伦比亚特区,1987年。

技术熟练的骑自行车者更喜欢在街道系统中与汽车并行，至于单独的自行车道或者共享车道哪种方式对于他们更安全、更舒适，这里有一些争论[172]。但无论如何，两者都是更倾向于共享标准宽度车道[173]。佛罗里达州的许多城市和县正在构建有着自行车道或更宽的外侧车道的城市干道。

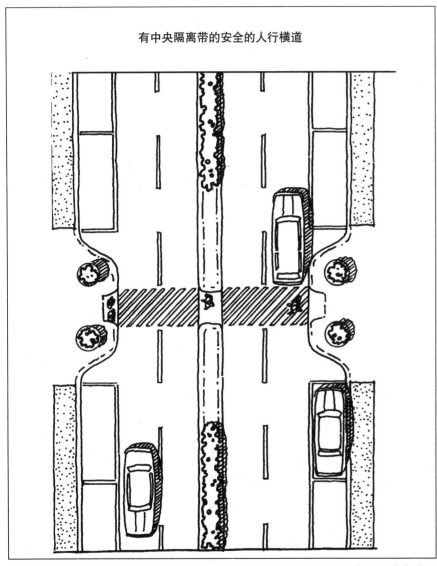

图片来源：引自佛罗里达州交通部（FDOT），适于步行的社区——完成一个有效的项目的12个步骤，塔拉哈西，1993年。

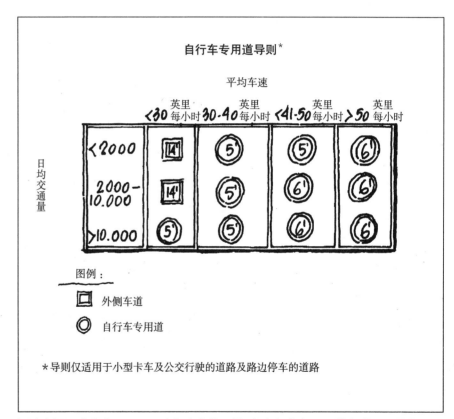

图片来源：改编自 W·C·威尔金森等，《顺应自行车交通的特定道路设计方法》，联邦公路管理局，华盛顿哥伦比亚特区，1994年。

另一个市场是儿童和成人休闲自行车，他们的数量远远多于高技能的成人骑自行车者，比例高达20%[174]。这个不需技能的大群体必须在脱离高速和大容量交通的地方骑车。几乎所有"大规模骑自行车上学"的人都会选择单独的自行车道和自行小路或少量住宅街道[175]。在佛罗里达的一些地方，骑自行车是主要的交通方式，如在盖恩斯维尔和基韦斯特，有许多自行车道、自行车小路和大量低洼的街道并联干道。

最近，交通工程师协会联合起来，总结了主要国家和地区的自行车专用道路标准和规格[176]。文件内容远远超出了基本的国家参考自行车设施指南[177]，这是十分有价值的做法。

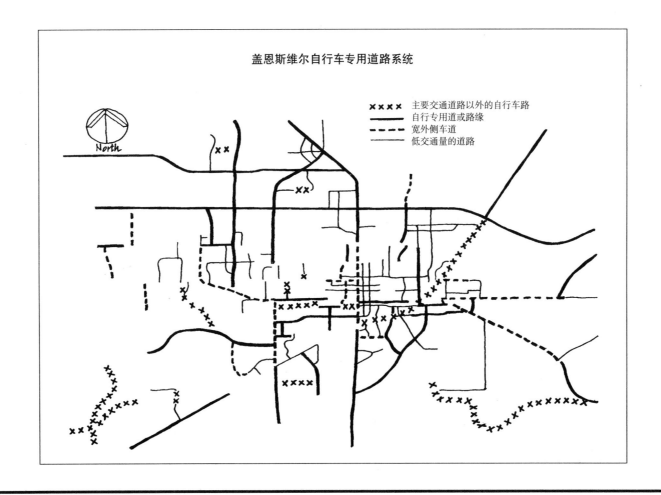

使旅行有趣

开车通常只是为了到达目的地，而步行和骑自行车出行不仅如此还更注重旅途的体验。因此，在设计高速道路时，要坚持简单性和开放性；在设计人行街道时，要保持丰富性和可视性[178]。

要想吸引到行人，街道不仅应该是简单的运动通道，也要是一个空间，这个空间被定义为良好的公共空间。在城市地区，空间框架是由建筑立面创造并从视觉上围合出来的。在郊区，空间有着更大的发展余地，连续的行道树和树冠可以创建出一个有类似效果的空间。特殊的铺路材料、街道家具、公共艺术、公园、广场也使街道环境有更多的居室气氛，增加空间感。

要想吸引到行人，街道设计必须符合人的尺度而不是汽车尺度。街区应该较短（如果过长，应以小巷或其他的通道分隔开）；街道应该相对狭窄（如果宽度超过两个车道以上，应以宽的中央种植带分隔成就像两个单行道一样）；建筑应该是小尺度（或如果较大，应以多个入口连通）；墙和栅栏应该以对齐和装饰的变化减弱其冗长感；停车区域也应该被各种各样的景观岛、建筑附加物或其他视觉分隔物分隔开。

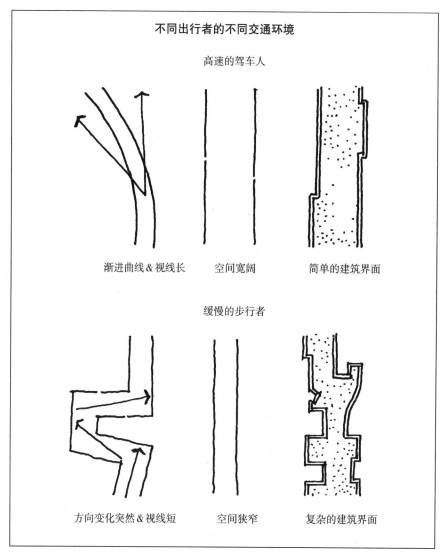

图片来源：引自 A·拉波波特．《步行街的应用：文化与认知》A·V·莫顿编，公众使用的公共街道。哥伦比亚大学出版社，纽约，1991 年，© 1991 由哥伦比亚大学出版社，版权人授权转载。

街道空间限定良好和限定较差的对比

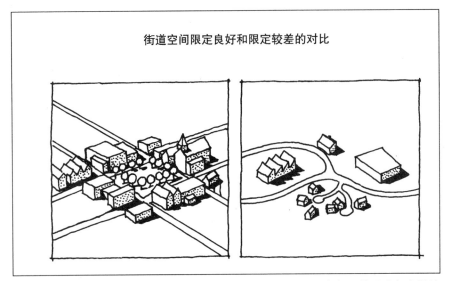

图片来源：M·索斯沃斯和P·M·欧文斯，《大都市地区的演变：关于城市边界地区的社区、邻里单位和街道形式的研究》美国规划协会期刊，59卷，1993年。

人行和车行街区的对比

旧金山，加利福尼亚州　　　　尔湾市，加利福尼亚州

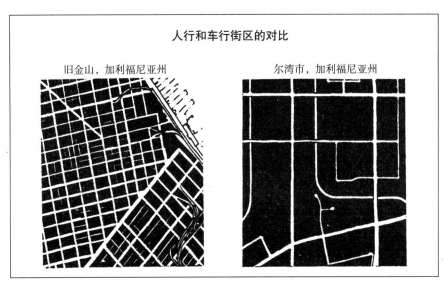

图片来源：A·B·雅各布斯，伟大的街道，麻省理工学院出版社，1993年，剑桥，马萨诸塞州。

人行和车行尺度的建筑

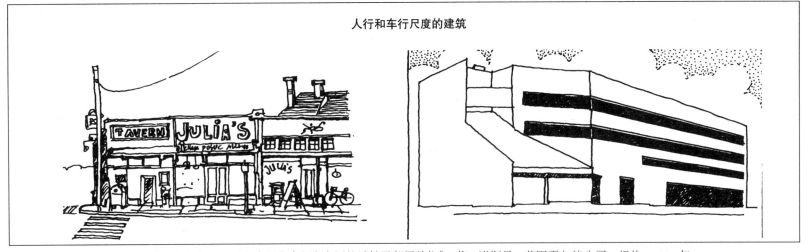

图片来源：R·K·尤特曼，《迎合行人——适宜步行和自行车交通的城镇及邻里单位》，范·诺斯丹·莱因霍尔德公司，纽约，1984年。

要想吸引到行人，环境中必须存在丰富的人群活动，因为人们最喜欢与人互动；土地使用率必须足够高，再加上土地使用功能充分混合，才能支持行人步行过程中的实用目的性。狭窄的前路，低洼的地面可以作为特别好的活动场地，就像设计师对于购物中心的作用一样。

1991年，漫步杂志列出了全美排名前10位适宜步行的城市[179]。这些城市被选中的原因，在某种程度上，源于他们的紧凑发展模式、拓宽人行道和建设汽车禁止通行区等做法。但该杂志正在寻找这之外的原因，具体地说，是一个特殊的因素——"让景色在人行道上细细观赏比在汽车上匆匆浏览更吸引人。"这个特质据说来源于行人尺度的商店、各类建筑、被精力充沛的街边小贩烘托出的明快的街头生活、艺人和橱窗前的购物者。

由于有着更快的出行速度，骑自行车者不像行人需要那么多的可视外立面、人群方式和人群活动，但他们也会被舒适的环境和有趣的景色吸引。1990年，《自行车》杂志评选的美国北部十大自行车城市中[180]，盖恩斯维尔排名第6。这些城市的共同点是拥有相当长的自行车道——并不只是自行车行车道或加宽的路缘车道，而是在多数情况下，景区会为业余车手提供自行车道。盖恩斯维尔的三个"行车路线"就是例子：皮内拉斯线路连接了圣彼得堡到克利尔沃特再到塔彭斯普林斯，它让这些城市拥有国内顶级的自行车线路之一；每月10万人使用这条线路，其中大约三分之一的人是去工作，购物或其他出行目的。

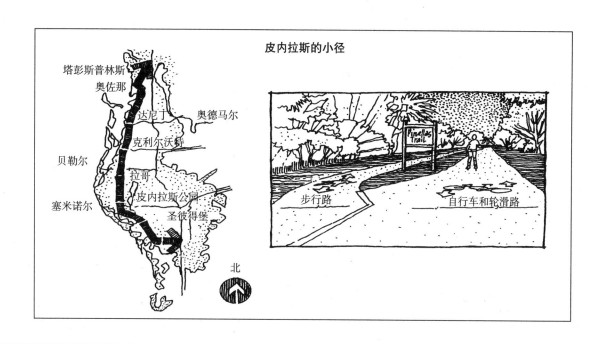

交通减速

街道环境承受了极大的交通量和交通速度的增长[181]。排列成一条线停放的汽车可以作为一个缓冲带，其作用就像一排行道树或路灯一样。如果有这条缓冲带，人行道可以设置在距道路远一些的位置；但是即使有一个缓冲，如果人行道坐落在一个高速、高容量的大道旁，它也不会吸引到行人。

交通减速使交通工具总是维持在中等速度移动。短途路段、T型交叉口、路边停车、路面铺砖、曲折的曲线、窄巷以及人行横道的增加只是使交通静化的可行措施中的一小部分。欧式交通静化率先在欧洲实行并在英国和澳大利亚推广，直到几年前，它仍未被美国北部的规划师和工程师熟知[182]。而现在它是大量文章、书籍和即将到来的交通工程师协会举办的国际会议的主题[183]，更多关于交通减速的最佳开发实践——设计、布置及各种措施的影响——都在这本指南手册中[184]。

美国北部的许多城市已经转向运用交通静化以及在老年社区中构建直通式交通来应对超速问题。劳德代尔堡拨给10个社区各10万美元用于这个方案中设施的改进，并最终相对佛罗里达的其他地方采取了更多的措施。盖恩斯维尔已经在其社区中布置了迷你交通圈，并关闭了约15条住宅区的街道。萨拉索塔市给社区提供了一个交通减速选项的范围，包括减速带、速度表、路段宽度缩减和交通分流。

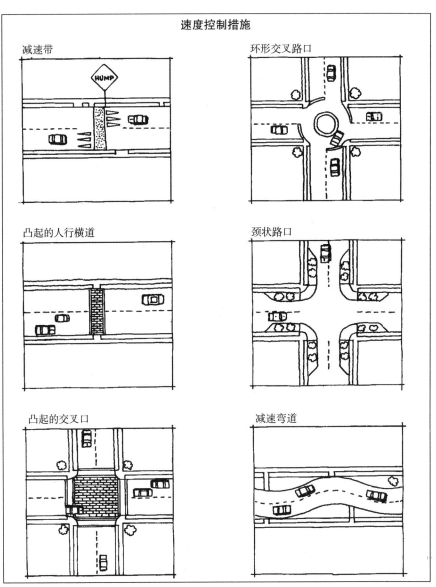

图片来源：引自科罗拉多州博尔德市缓解邻里单位交通项目——工具措施，未更新。

佛罗里达首次为贝莱尔镇拟定了一个覆盖全区的交通减速计划[185]。当地重点组织强调他们希望美化社区的同时静化交通的目标；保持社区街道对贝莱尔相邻镇的开放，但要迫使邻镇尊重当地的速度限制，以避免严厉的减速带等措施，惩罚违反速度限制的居民。这个计划决定采用突出环形路、提高路口、缩减单车道路段宽度以及其他从欧洲和澳大利亚引进的措施[186]。配备铺路表面信号标识和景观融合，这些措施保证了社区视觉效果的统一，从而减缓交通速度。

至少对于当地的街道来说，佛罗里达州是交通静化的早期支持者之一。佛罗里达的交通发展实践已经是其第三项的交通实践，"充分使用交通静化措施。"下一版的佛罗里达标准街道设计手册将包含一章关于街道交通静化的内容[187]。

指定地点的缓冲居住区交通的措施

	劳德代尔堡	贝茨维尔	那不勒斯	萨拉索塔	塔拉哈西	坦帕布
速度控制措施						
标准减速带	■	❑		■		■
连续减速带／时速表	■	❑	❑		■	
环形交叉路口					❑	
减速带	■				■	■
凸起			■			
减速路						
凸起的路口		❑				
交通量控制措施						
封闭街区	■			■		■
完全分流	■		❑			
部分分流	■		❑	❑		■
单行道		■				■
缓冲区域交通	■			■		

■ 措施到位　❑ 建议措施

图片来源：作者于1996年末的调查。

第九章　不只是速度
——新一代交通水平评价指标和方法

现在，从传统的角度来看，交通专家致力于研究的最终目标是要将人口尽可能快速、高效地疏散到城市周边……但是，这是没有解决方案的……城市应该是目的而非一种手段。

柯克帕特里克·塞尔[189]

我们可以发现，对在土地利用及交通运输规划方面的"范例转变"需要不断被人提及[190]。如果我们在规划方面需要范例的转变，交通运输系统评价也同样需要范例转变。总之，我们不应该过于强调机动车的车速，而是应该更多地强调人们的交通需求得到了多大程度上的满足。

交通范例转变

交通系统规划及实践长期使用道路服务水平这一名词。道路服务水平评价像学生的成绩单一样，分为 A 到 F 几个等级。LOS A 代表交通畅通，LOS F 代表严重的交通堵塞。交通规划师和工程师一心一意地追求好"成绩"。

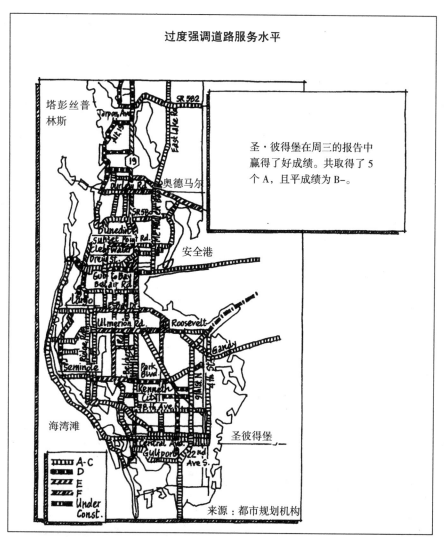

图片来源："地区道路取得了长足的进步"，圣彼得堡时报，1991年2月14日。

需要注意的是，从广义来讲，道路服务水平可以替代速度评价[191]。市区和郊区主干道的平均通行速度是一个简单函数[192]。其他类型的道路与速度的关系不那么直接却关系密切。一旦确定了道路的设计速度，其服务水平就成为与平均交通速度相关的简单函数[193]。

在进行新的道路规划或道路拓宽时，道路服务水平无可厚非的将成为首要考虑因素。道路设施的用途毕竟是实现交通的流动。

城市发展管理是另一回事。如何最好地利用现有设施与重新建设这些设施一样重要。节约能源、邻里保护、市中心振兴和其他公共目的都在与实现畅通无阻的交通这一愿望争夺优先权。

由于一心一意地追求交通速度，遏制城市蔓延这一特别重要的公共目标往往被忽视。通过提高交通速度可以增加出行距离[194]。城市开发能够并也确实使城市变得越来越分散。其他研究也对易受其他公共目标影响的新土地利用和交通运输范式进行了描述和说明[195]。

干路服务水平

干路等级	I	II	III
服务水平	车辆平均行驶速度（英里每小时）		
A	≥ 35	≥ 30	≥ 25
B	≥ 28	≥ 24	≥ 19
C	≥ 22	≥ 18	≥ 13
D	≥ 17	≥ 14	≥ 9
E	≥ 13	≥ 10	≥ 7
F	< 13	< 10	< 7

图片来源：交通运输研究委员会、交通道路容量手册特别报告209，第三版，表11-1. © 交通运输研究委员会，国家研究理事会，1994，华盛顿哥伦比亚特区。

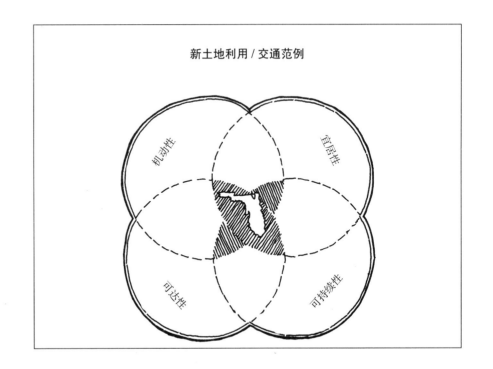

新土地利用/交通范例

州和联邦法律的变化

交通范式的转变也已经随着州和联邦法律的变化而展开。1993年佛罗里达州城市发展管理法允许当地政府将城市填充区和城市复兴区（交通特殊区域或TCEAs）排除在道路服务等级标准之外[196]。这一变化应该有助于消除一些对于城市外围发展的偏重。在紧凑的交通特殊区域或TCEAs内部，当地政府也可以以区域范围为基础（而不是习惯采用的以地段为基础）对道路服务水平进行评价[197]。这一措施增加了交通的灵活性，因此，州政府希望采用交通系统管理（TSM）手段，实施出行需求管理（TDM）项目，并且鼓励跨地区的合作应用。

联邦洁净空气法1990年修正案要求各州制定计划，以使污染地区达到国家空气质量标准。车辆行驶里程（VMT）、行车车次和平均出行速度这三种交通评价指标在这些计划及相关的空气质量检测中发挥着关键的作用[198]。如果未达到计划中制定的目标水平，预报和跟踪监测车辆行驶里程（VMT）、行车车次、平均出行速度以及一些其他控制措施将会自动启用。在臭氧浓度和一氧化碳浓度较高的区域，计划必须包括充足的交通管制措施（TCMs），以抵消由于车辆行驶里程（VMT）和行车车次增长所带来的排放。作为空气质量预测的基础，联邦排放模型用平均出行速度来估算排放因子（以克每英里为单位），排放因子再乘以车辆行驶里程（VMT）便计算得出总排放水平。

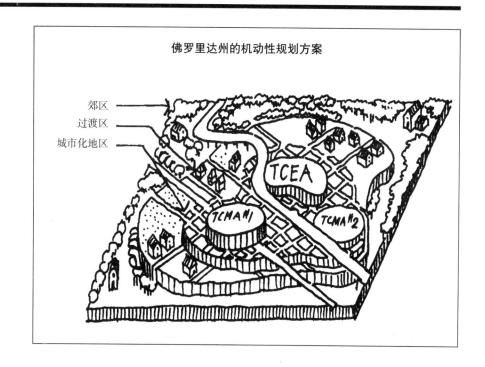

佛罗里达州的机动性规划方案

郊区
过渡区
城市化地区

1991年联邦综合地面交通效率法案要求各州和大都市规划机构制定交通堵塞管理系统。这一系统必须包括评价指标和执行监督措施。联邦政府已经提供了从平均出行时间到HOV车道的使用人数等一系列可能的评价指标[199]。至于应该采取哪些措施，联邦导则仅仅指出测评的重点在于人的交通指标，而非车辆指标[200]。

在 ISTEA 的实施中，佛罗里达州正在进行并要求其城市化地区对高速公路和交通运输情况进行评价[201]。同时也鼓励对自行车和行人交通设施进行评价。

总之，法律法规的变化正使得佛罗里达州和全美不再视车辆行驶速度为交通规划的全部或者终点。这是我们首次在多种模式的语境下讨论机动性，也是我们首次认为应该重视减少交通流量而非增大交通流量。在这样的背景下，当地政府和都市规划组织在进行交通评价指标选择时具有充分的创新性。

来自国家政府的导则

最近几篇关于交通评价的文章和报告都是在州和联邦法律调整的背景下产生的（或者是在此背景的促进下产生的）[202]。文章和报告回顾了一些可能的交通评价方法和指标，下述为常用的评价指标和方法[203]。

- 不同层次的分析需要不同的评价指标和方法。一些指标和方法非常适用于单独的设施评价，还有一些适用于交通廊道的评价，另外一些则适用于地区性的交通网络评价。

- 对出行者来说，最重要的是出行交通体验，而非交通设施条件。举例来说，与平均速度计算出的交通流量/容量比相比，平均车速是一个更好的评价指标。

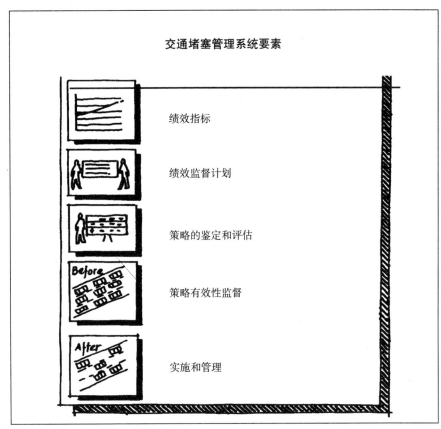

图片来源：JHK 及合作单位，针对技术人员的交通堵塞管理，3 天的培训课程．联邦高速公路管理局，华盛顿特区，1994 年。

- 在选定交通模式的情况下，机动性必须要在多种交通模式中进行评价。我们可以结合高速公路、交通转换和步行评价指标，或者不同交通模式的指标来达到这一目标。

- 可达性必须要纳入某一层面的交通分析中。可达性（而不是机动性）最终决定了出行者目的地和出行时间。

- 对决策者来说，交通评价指标和方法越简单易懂用处就越大。

统一的指标评价方法

接下来，我们要从一般性概念性导则跨越到一系列具体的评价指标和方法。

系统性目标
发展一个统一的评价指标和方法系统来源于一个系统性的目标。两个最主要的目标因其可操作性轻而易举的脱颖而出，其与 ISTEA、洁净空气法和 1993 年佛罗里达州城市发展管理法相辅相成。

一个值得追求的目标是在区域或本地区范围内尽可能地减少车辆行驶里程（VMT）或人均车辆行驶里程（VMT）。

洁净空气法将车辆行驶里程（VMT）列为臭氧和一氧化碳浓度较高地区的主要交通评价指标。车辆行驶里程（VMT）对城市发展管理也是一个简单却重要的指标[204]。如果进行土地混合利用，车辆行驶里程（VMT）将会降低；如果路网设计能够四通八达，车辆行驶里程（VMT）将会降低；如果很好地实施了交通换乘和拼车等措施，车辆行驶里程（VMT）将会降低。发展需要一个底线，因此，加利福尼亚州空气资源委员会制定了一项目标，即在污染地区的车辆行驶里程（VMT）增长率不高于污染的增长率（人均 VMT 因此趋于平缓）。同样，为使俄勒冈州四个最大的都市地区的人均车辆行驶里程（VMT）在 20 年内减少 10%，俄勒冈州土地保护与发展委员会应运而生[205]。

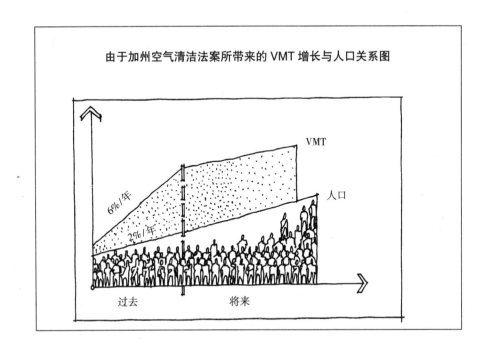

另外一个值得追求的目标是减少车辆行驶时间（VHT），或者区域和社区范围内的人均VHT。与车辆行驶里程（VMT）相比，车辆行驶时间（VHT）具有很大的优势。车辆行驶时间（VHT）可以用来评价交通堵塞的程度，在其他变量相同的情况下，道路交通堵塞越严重，车辆行驶时间（VHT）就越长。车辆行驶时间（VHT）与车辆的尾气排放之间的关系要比车辆行驶里程（VMT）与之的关系更加简单和直接。你可以发现，每英里车辆排放的下降（在一定程度上）与车速相关，因此，车辆行驶里程（VMT）的下降未必会使车辆排放下降，事实上，这完全取决于车辆平均速度的影响程度。同时，车辆每小时的排放量则在很大程度上取决于车速，任何车辆行驶时间（VHT）的降低都会带来排放量的减少。

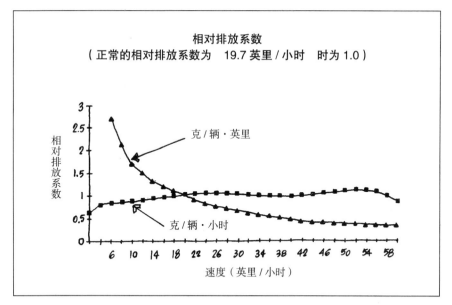

图片来源：用于碳氢化合物和一氧化碳的排放图，引自L·E·盖茨，"加州的方法来评估机动车空气污染物排放量"，该论文发表于第82届APCA/AWMA年会，1989年。

因此，我们建议将尽可能减少车辆行驶时间（VHT）作为一个系统性的目标。接下来我们将讨论如何运用这一指标评价。

区域和本地区

一些区域和地区性的指标都是在车辆行驶时间（VHT）计算公式的基础上自然发展出来的：

$$\text{VHT/人} = \frac{\text{平均出行频率} \times \text{平均出行路程} \times (1-\text{平均非机动车出行方式比例})}{\text{平均车辆利用率} \times \text{平均车辆行驶速度}}$$

公式右侧为所需的指标数据。这些指标全都满足上述的一般性导则要求（即简单、易于理解、适用于多种模式等），最大的缺点在于该地区数据的可用性。

所有的指标数据都可以通过家庭出行调查进行估算，但这种调查成本较高，且只有在区域交通模式更新时才能进行。因此，利用同一地区的交通出行模式，定期进行车辆行驶时间（VHT）估算是最好的也是仅有的可能方法。

大都市规划组织、地区性规划委员会、当地的交通工程部门和咨询公司经常使用这一模型。作为成果标准的一部分，他们要估算车辆行驶时间（VHT）、平均出行距离和车辆平均行驶速度。

区域性出行模式适用于现在或未来多年的发展。"城市形态"研究、可能的土地利用方案或各类分析研究、可能的交通运输改善方式等均可应用这一模式。可以按照或不按照发展建议来实施这些模式，并就城市开发对区域内车辆行驶时间（VHT）、平均出行距离和车辆平均行驶速度的影响进行评估。区域出行模式已经在许多地区用于对大型开发项目的影响进行评估，区别在于指标底线是用来推算区域内的车辆出行时间（VHT），而不是推算单个道路的服务水平。

必须指出这些模式中的两个局限性[206]。首先，根据这些模式进行的估计和预测只能是粗略的，尤其是对于单独的交通设施而言，但如果将各个设施的估算汇集在一起计算地区总量时，这一结果则更为可靠。其次，一些"软措施"对于这些模式的影响微弱，但却可能影响车辆行驶时间（VHT）方程中的两个指标要素：平均车辆利用率和平均非机动车出行比例。这些模式也不能代表交通需求管理（TDM）计划、自行车和步行设施改善、小范围内土地综合利用等项目的全部。我们也注意到，区域性的交通模式在不断的更新发展中（在同一时间进行的其他几个区域性和全国性的研究项目中）[207]。

交通廊道和活动中心

对于交通廊道和活动中心来说，VHT计算公式中的平均车辆行驶速度、平均车辆利用率和平均非机动车出行比例是与之关系最密切的两个数据指标。平均车辆利用率与高速公路交通廊道尤其相关，这些交通廊道缺少HOV车道且交通堵塞严重，因此拼车在这些地方更具有吸引力。平均非机动车出行比例与大都市地区的活动中心尤其相关，这些地区通常是高密度的土地混合利用并且有很好的步行设施，因此使得步行交通更具吸引力。

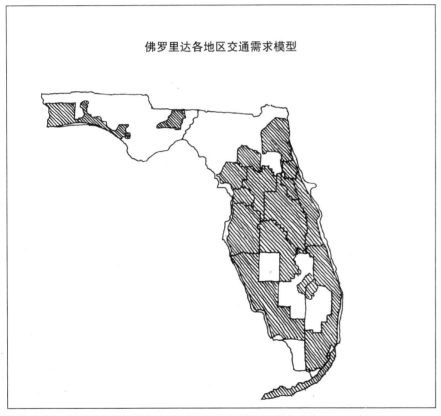

图片来源：佛罗里达州交通运输部（FDOT）系统规划办公室，1994年。

与平均车辆行驶速度相关的因素无处不在。由于没有标准的计算方法，全国范围内的地区都逐步发展起来了各自区域内的交通设施服务水平的评价方法[208]。大部分地区已经将平均交通流量/容量比作为区域范围内交通服务水平评价的基础。交通流量是几类交通设施的总计，交通容量是相同的几类交通设施的总计，而前者与后者的比值即为平均交通流量/容量比。这一方法已经被广泛应用：华盛顿的贝尔维尤、加利福尼亚的圣何塞等次级地区的道路交叉口评价；华盛顿国王郡、马里兰州的蒙哥马利郡等次级地区的道路分段评价；佛罗里达橘郡的交通廊道的平行道路评价；华盛顿皮尔斯县交叉口"屏线"的评价[209]。在此基础上的一个变体——利用人行而不是车行来进行交通流量和容量测算，已经被应用于迈阿密多种交通廊道模式的评价中[210]。

一个潜在的区域范围内道路服务水平的评价指标是平均车辆行驶速度。这一指标比平均交通流量/容量比更能直接地进行评价，也更加符合1985年公路容量手册的要求（其中使用了其他更为直接的评价指标，舍弃了交通流量/容量比这一指标）。在概念层面上，这是从计算主干路平均车速（自1985年公路容量手册更新以来已经开始实际应用）到计算交通廊道或活动中心内平均车速（暂时未被采纳，但在城市发展管理和交通堵塞管理的背景下十分合理）的一小步转变。

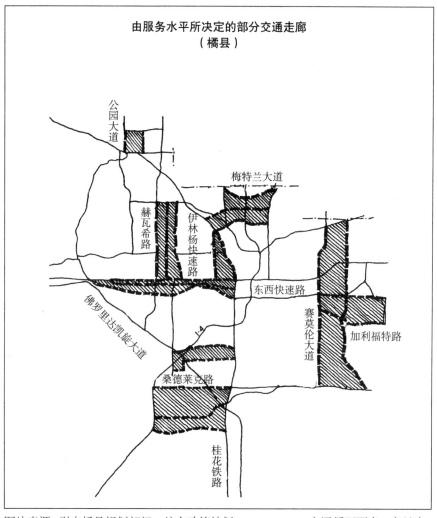

图片来源：引自橘县规划部门，综合政策计划—1990~2010—交通循环要素，奥兰多，佛罗里达州，1992年。

因为车辆行驶速度的急剧下降与各个独立的部门息息相关，因此地方政府将有充足的激励措施来解决本地区的交通问题。然而，即使整个系统的投资更注重成本效益，他们也不会断然切断资金投入，迫使各个道路连接起来以达到最低服务水平。

单独的设施

在 VHT 方程中唯一与单独的道路相关的变量是车辆平均行驶速度，或者是另一种说法——道路服务水平。国内有些人建议将单条道路的评价指标换成以交通延误时间为基础的指标。无论使用延误时间这一指标有多大的理论优势，道路服务水平的评价都拥有巨大的实践优势——熟悉。全国 90% 的交通机构使用道路服务水平作为交通堵塞情况的评价指标，没有其他指标能够被如此广泛的使用[211]。在实行城市发展管理下的各州，当地政府对道路服务水平是再熟悉不过了。

道路服务水平标准已经被写进了大量的公共设施条例和几个州的律例中[212]。因此，无论将该指标换成任何指标都很难达到预期效果，最好的情况也只是达到部分效果。

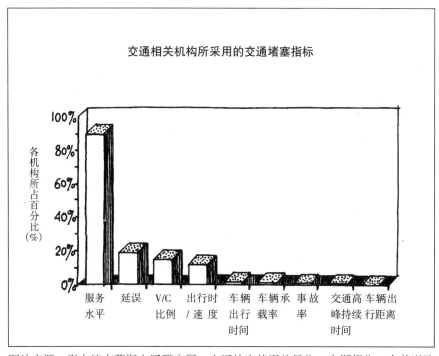

图片来源：引自德克萨斯交通研究所，交通堵塞状况的量化—中期报告。全美道路合作研究项目报告，交通研究委员会，华盛顿哥伦比亚特区，1992。

可变的服务标准

如果仍将车辆平均行驶速度或道路服务水平作为单条道路的评价指标，考虑到中心地区越来越多的交通堵塞，其比较标准必须是可变的。否则，道路服务水平评价标准可能会在无意中推动城市向容纳能力强的外围地区发展，从而促进了城市的无序蔓延。

地区内目的地与出发地之间的相对可达性是建立可变的评价标准的客观基础。出行距离越短、机动交通时间越短，可达性就越好[213]。城市核心区、高密度的交通廊道、紧凑的市郊中心区的交通可能会比偏远地区更加拥堵，但仍然提供了与目的地之间很好的可达性。缺乏机动性（比如车辆行驶速度较慢）这一问题也由于出行距离的缩短而抵消了。

服务标准的可变性可以通过两种方式实现。可以用区域交通模型或交通调查来估算区域内各分区的平均出行距离，在各分区建立较低级别的服务标准，以便缩短出行距离。或者可以用区域交通模型估算区域内各个分区的可达性，在这些地区建立较低级别的服务标准，进而提高可达性指数。可达性指数反映了向区域外围移动的交通中就业地点和其他出行目的地的分布情况，与偏远的目的地相比，该地区周边的出行目的地的权重更大[214]。

案例

从其精神宗旨上来说，今天的一些评价指标和方法系统更像是一个理想化的系统。奥兰多市使用一个区域范围的服务水平指标来评价城市中心区的道路性能。具体而言，总行车里程的百分比等于或高于某一服务水平标准时，则被监测和判定是违背了等于或高于85%的这一目标。虽然这不如车辆平均行驶速度这一指标有用，但只要将道路网络作为一个整体，行车里程百分比这一指标至少可以让一些局部交通堵塞地区充分发挥其道路交通性能。

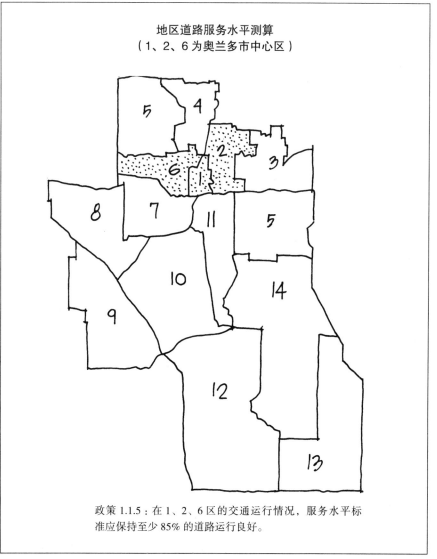

政策1.1.5：在1、2、6区的交通运行情况，服务水平标准应保持至少85%的道路运行良好。

图片来源：奥兰多城交通运行要素，1991年8月12日获批。

此外，奥兰多市将平均车辆利用率和/或出行模式比例，连同道路服务水平一起进行指标评价，以指定相应的活动中心和交通廊道。为了达到车辆利用率和出行模式比例标准，政府采取了一系列举措，如在中心区和交通廊道沿线地区采取最低密度和强度的土地开发及土地混合利用；增加中心区内和中心区之间的交通换乘频率；征收专项税为步行交通设施和地区内部通勤交通服务提供资金。

奥兰多市在1997年进行了总体规划修编，计划加入车辆行驶里程（VMT）这一指标作为不同用地功能的评价。这一变化由基于信息技术的"查询"系统支持。该系统将使开发商能够快速查询他们的规划是否符合城市标准，配合VMT这一指标制定给予交通政策上的奖励措施，鼓励有碍交通发展的地区内的项目自觉地转换成其他开发模式。我们的想法是，未来对优秀的土地混合利用项目的奖励措施将不仅仅局限于开发审批方面，也会在征收开发影响费方面给予优惠。

结束语

土地利用——交通系统是公认的一个各个要素相互依存的"系统"（尽管很少进行这方面的规划和管理）。这涉及了交通服务评价指标和方法。理想情况下，评价指标和方法将反映土地利用模式和交通网络的效率，表现出这一系统的多种模式性质，将连接性道路和交通节点作为系统的一部分。本章已经做出了一定的尝试，尽管只是初步工作，但希望能够基于上述讨论制定一套系统的交通水平评价指标和方法。

注释

1 Select Committee on Roads, *Report to Legislative Council Covering Florida Primary Roads*, Legislative Reference Bureau, Tallahassee, Fla., 1954, p. 2.

2 Department of Community Affairs (DCA), *Focus on Mobility: An Initiative of the Department of Community Affairs and Transportation*, Tallahassee, Fla., 1991, p. 1.

3 A.E. Pisarski, *Travel Behavior Issues in the 90's*, Federal Highway Administration, Washington, D.C., 1992, p. 13.

4 A. Downs, "The Law of Peak-Hour Expressway Congestion," *Traffic Quarterly*, Vol. 16, 1962, pp. 393-409. Also see R.L. Morris, "Traffic as a Function of Supply and Demand," *Traffic Quarterly*, Vol. 31, 1977, pp. 591-603; D.J. Holden, "Wardrop's Third Principle: Urban Traffic Congestion and Traffic Policy," *Journal of Transport Economics and Policy*, Vol.23, 1989, pp. 239-262; and A. Downs, *Stuck in Traffic: Coping with Peak-Hour Traffic Congestion*, The Brookings Institution, Washington, D.C., 1992, pp. 26-33.

5 M. Hansen, "Do New Highways Generate Traffic?" *Access*, Vol. 7, Fall 1995, pp. 16-22. The subject of induced travel is fraught with controversy. See R. Kitamura, "The Effects of Added Transportation Capacity on Travel: A Review of Theoretical and Empirical Results," in G. Shunk (ed.), *The Effects of Added Transportation Capacity*, Technology Sharing Program, U.S. Department of Transportation, Washington, D.C., 1991, 79-95; M. Hansen et al., *The Air Quality Impacts of Urban Highway Capacity Expansion: Traffic Generation and Land Use Change*, Institute of Transportation Studies, University of California at Berkeley, 1993; R.G. Dowling et al., *Effects of Increased Highway Capacity on Travel Behavior*, California Air Resources Board, Sacramento, Calif., 1994; H. Cohen, "Review of Empirical Studies of Induced Traffic," in *Expanding Metropolitan Highways: Implications for Air Quality and Energy Use*, Special Report 245, Transportation Research Board, National Academy Press, Washington, D.C., 1995, pp. 295-309; Committee for the Study of Impacts of Highway Capacity Improvements on Air Quality and Energy Consumption, "Travel Demand," in *Expanding Metropolitan Highways: Implications for Air Quality and Energy Use*, Special Report 245, Transportation Research Board, National Academy Press, Washington, D.C., 1995, pp. 138-173; and M. Replogle, "Minority Statement," in *Expanding Metropolitan Highways: Implications for Air Quality and Energy Use*, Special Report 245, Transportation Research Board, National Academy Press, Washington, D.C., 1995, pp. 354-380.

6 These figures represent an average of cost estimates from three sources, one (FHWA) with relatively high variable and low fixed costs, the others the reverse (AAA and AAMA). Jack Faucett Associates, *The Costs of Owning and Operating Automobiles, Vans and Light Trucks: 1991*, Federal Highway Administration, Washington, D.C., 1992; American Automobile Association (AAA), *Your Driving Costs*, Heathrow, Fla., 1993; and American Automobile Manufacturers Association (AAMA), *Motor Vehicle Facts & Figures '94*, Detroit, 1994, p. 54.

7 M. Cameron, *Transportation Efficiency: Tackling Southern California's Air Pollution and Congestion*, Environmental Defense Fund, Oakland, Calif., 1991, p. 21; B.M. Faigin, "The Costs of Motor Vehicle Injuries," *Auto & Traffic Safety*, Vol. 1, No. 1, 1991, pp. 2-9; H.M. Hubbard, "The Real Cost of Energy," *Scientific American*, Vol. 264, April 1991, pp. 36-40; T. Miller, *The Costs of Highway Crashes*, Federal Highway Administration, Washington, D.C., 1991; L.J. Blincoe and B.M. Faigin, *The Economic Cost of Motor Vehicle Crashes, 1990*, National Highway Traffic Safety Administration, Washington, D.C., 1992; M.E. Hanson, "Automobile Subsidies and Land Use: Estimates and Policy Responses," *Journal of the American Planning Association*, Vol. 58, 1992, pp. 60-71; J.J. MacKenzie, R.C. Dower, and D.T. Chen, *The Going Rate: What It Really Costs to Drive*, World Resources Institute, Washington, D.C., 1992, pp. 10-19; K.A. Small, *Urban Transportation Economics*, Harwood Academic Publishers, Chur, Switzerland, 1992, pp. 75-85; R.W. Willson, *Suburban Parking Economics and Policy: Case Studies of Office Worksites in Southern California*, Technology Sharing Program, U.S. Department of Transportation, Washington, D.C., 1992, pp. 23-25; P. Miller and J. Moffet, *The Price of Mobility: Uncovering the Hidden Costs of Transportation*, Natural Resources Defense Council, Washington, D.C., 1993, pp. 14-62; Apogee Research, Inc., *The Costs of Transportation: Final Report*, Conservation Law Foundation, Boston, 1994, pp. 82-162; T. Moore and P. Thorsnes, *The Transportation/Land Use Connection*, American Planning Association, Chicago, 1994, p. 48; Office of Technology Assessment (OTA), *Saving Energy in U.S. Transportation*, Congress of the United States, Washington, D.C., 1994, pp. 98-134; M.K. Teets, *Bulletin: Receipts and Disbursements for Highways 1989-1992*, Federal Highway Administration, Washington, D.C., 1994, pp. IV-6 and V-115; Committee for Study on Urban Transportation Congestion Pricing, *Curbing Gridlock: Peak-Period Fees to Relieve Congestion—Volume 1*, Special Report 242, Transportation Research Board, Washington, D.C., 1994, Appendix B; E. Verhoef, "External Effects and Social Costs of Road Transport," *Transportation Research A*, Vol. 2A, 1994, pp. 273-287; D.B. Lee, "Full Cost

Pricing of Highways," *Transportation Research Record 1518*, 1996, pp. 57-64; T. Litman, *Transportation Cost Analysis: Techniques, Estimates and Implications*, Victoria Transport Policy Institute, Victoria, British Columbia, 1995, pp. 3.0-1 through 3.16-2; K.A. Small and C. Kazimi, "On the Costs of Air Pollution from Motor Vehicles," *Journal of Transport Economics and Policy*, Vol. 29, 1995, pp. 7-32; M.A. Delucchi, "Total Cost of Motor-Vehicle Use," *Access*, Vol. 8, Spring 1996, pp. 7-13; and J. Qin et al., "Evaluating Full Costs of Urban Passenger Transportation," paper presented at the 75th Annual Meeting, Transportation Research Board, Washington, D.C., 1996.

8 Cameron, op. cit., p. 21; MacKenzie et al., op. cit., p. 24; and Moore and Thorsnes, op. cit., p. 48. It is occasionally argued that the auto-highway system produces social benefits (external to the market and uncompensated) that somehow offset the social costs of the system (also external to the market and uncompensated). This possibility is considered and neatly dismissed in W. Rothengatter, "Do External Benefits Compensate for External Costs of Transport?" *Transportation Research A*, Vol. 28A, 1994, pp. 321-328. Likewise, it is occasionally suggested that technological fixes (cleaner vehicle) will save us from the rising social costs of the auto-highway system. This possibility is discounted in K.M. Gwilliam and H. Geerlings, "New Technologies and Their Potential to Reduce the Environmental Impact of Transportation," *Transportation Research A*, Vol. 28A, 1994, pp. 307-319.

9 Florida Department of Transportation (FDOT), *Florida Pedestrian Safety Plan*, Tallahassee, 1992, p. I-5.

10 D. Popenoe, "Urban Sprawl: Some Neglected Sociological Considerations," *Sociology and Social Research*, Vol. 63, 1979, pp. 255-268.

11 K.H. Schaeffer and E. Sclar, *Access for All*, Penguin Books, Baltimore, 1975; D. Popenoe, *The Suburban Environment*, University of Chicago Press, Chicago, 1977, pp. 193-201; M. Berg and E.A. Medrich, "Children in Four Neighborhoods: The Physical Environment and Its Effect on Play and Play Patterns," *Environment and Behavior*, Vol. 12, 1980, pp. 320-348; A.J. Millas, "Planning for the Elderly within the Context of a Neighborhood," *Ekistics*, Vol. 47, 1980, pp. 264-273; F.M. Carp, "Significance of Mobility for the Well-Being of the Elderly," in *Transportation in an Aging Society*, Special Report 218, Transportation Research Board, Washington, D.C., 1988, pp. 1-20; S. Rosenbloom, "The Mobility Needs of the Elderly," in *Transportation in an Aging Society*, Special Report 218, Transportation Research Board, Washington, D.C., 1988, pp. 21-71; M. Hillman, J. Adams, and J. Whitelegg, *One False Move...A Study of Children's Independent Mobility*, Policy Studies Institute, London, England, 1990, pp. 77-97; M.A. Hughes, "Employment Decentralization and Accessibility: A Strategy for Stimulating Regional Mobility," *Journal of the American Planning Association*, Vol. 57, 1991, pp. 288-298; J.F. Kain, "The Spatial Mismatch Hypothesis: Three Decades Later," *Housing Policy Debate*, Vol. 3, 1992, pp. 371-459; K.R. Ihlanfeldt, "Intra-urban Job Accessibility and Hispanic Youth Employment Rates," *Journal of Urban Economics*, Vol. 33, 1993, pp. 254-271; and R.W. Burchell and E. Schmeidler, "The Demographic and Social Difference Between Central Cities and Suburbs as They Relate to the Job Fulfillment of Urban Residents," paper presented at the National Conference on *Metropolitan America in Transition: Implications for Land Use and Transportation Planning*, Lincoln Institute of Land Policy, Cambridge, Mass., 1993.

12 Governor's Task Force on Urban Growth Patterns, *Final Report*, Florida Department of Community Affairs, Tallahassee, 1989, p. 45.

13 Subsections 163.3180(5)-(7), Florida Statutes; and Rule 9J-5.0055(5)-(6), Florida Administrative Code.

14 Subsection 163.3177(6)(j), Florida Statutes; and Rule 9J-5.019, Florida Administrative Code.

15 Under "conformity" provisions of the Clean Air Act, projected emission impacts of transportation plans must be consistent with "emission budgets" in air quality plans. For more on this requirement, see S. Siwek, "Conformity," in M. Franko (ed.), *ISTEA Planner's Workbook*, Surface Transportation Policy Project, Washington, D.C., 1994, pp. 79-100; J.P. Anderson and A.M. Howitt, "Clean Air Act SIPs, Sanctions, and Conformity, *Transportation Quarterly*, Vol. 49, Summer 1995, pp. 67-79; and R.P. Brodesky, "Air Quality Conformity Case Studies," *Transportation Research Record 1472*, 1995, pp. 1-8.

16 ISTEA has been assessed from various perspectives, and generally fared well: J. DiStefano and M. Raimi, *Five Years of Progress: 110 Communities Where ISTEA Is Making a Difference*, Surface Transportation Policy Project, Washington, D.C., 1996; J.H. Andrews, "Metro Power: With ISTEA, MPOs Have Found There's No Such Thing as Politics as Usual," *Planning*, Vol. 62, June 1996, pp. 8-12; Federal Transit Administration (FTA), *Planning, Developing, and Implementing Community-Sensitive Transit*, Livable Communities Initiative, Washington, D.C., 1996; T.L. Shaw, "The Impacts of ISTEA on Metropolitan Planning Practice," *ITE 1996 Compendium of Technical Papers*, Institute of Transportation Engineers, Washington, D.C., 1996, pp. 369-373; U.S. Advisory Commission on Intergovernmental Relations (ACIR), *Planning Progress: Addressing ISTEA Requirements in Metropolitan Planning Areas*, Washington, D.C., 1996; Surface Transportation Policy Project, "Five Years Later...," *Progress*,

Vol. 6, January 1997; and I.M. Chan (ed.), *Building on the Past: Traveling to the Future*, Federal Highway Administration/National Trust for Historic Preservation, Washington, D.C., undated. For a skeptic's view, see N. Denno, "ISTEA's Innovative Funding: Something Old, New and Borrowed," *Transportation Quarterly*, Vol. 48, 1994, pp. 275-285.

17 Florida has substituted a "mobility management process" for the federally mandated statewide congestion management system. Quoting the state's work plan: "By selecting 'mobility' with an emphasis on modal choice over 'congestion' (which most people primarily think of in terms of automobile traffic), performance measures must go beyond highway level of service measures and probably even beyond transit performance measures." Florida Department of Transportation (FDOT), *Florida's Mobility Management Process/Congestion Management System Work Plan*, Tallahassee, 1994, p. 51.

18 Department of Community Development, *Toward Managing Growth in Washington: A Guide to Community Visioning*, State of Washington, Olympia, 1991, p. 3.

19 The following language was added to s. 163.3167, Florida Statutes:

> Each local government is encouraged to articulate a vision of the future physical appearance and qualities of its community as a component of its local comprehensive plan. The vision should be developed through a collaborative planning process with meaningful public participation, and shall be adopted by the governing body of the jurisdiction.... The state land planning agency [DCA] shall serve as a clearinghouse for creating a community vision of the future and may utilize the Growth Management Trust Fund, created by s. 186.911, to provide grants to help pay the costs of local visioning programs. When a local vision of the future has been created, a local government should review its comprehensive plan, land development regulations, and capital improvement program to ensure that these instruments will help move the community toward its vision in a manner consistent with this act and with the state comprehensive plan.

20 Visioning techniques are described in Department of Community Development, op. cit.; R.L. Thomas, M.C. Means, and M.A. Grieve, *Taking Charge: How Communities Are Planning Their Futures*, International City Management Association, Washington, D.C., 1988; American Institute of Architects, *Design Your Town*, Washington, D.C., 1992; S.C. Ames (ed.), *Guide to Community Visioning: Hands on Information for Local Communities*, Oregon Visions Project, City of Sherwood, Oregon, 1993; K.J. Hirsch, "A Vision for the Florida Visioning Process," *Community Planning*, Vol. 2, April 1993, pp. 1, 4-5; Snohomish County Transportation Authority, *A Guide to Land Use and Public Transportation—Volume II: Applying the Concepts*, Lynnwood, Wash., 1993, pp. 1-21 through 1-27; and A.C. Nelessen, "Creating a Common Vision: Design by Democracy," *Visions for a New American Dream: Process, Principles, and an Ordinance to Plan and Design Small Communities*, American Planning Association, Chicago, 1994, pp. 81-103.

21 B. Ward, *Home of Man*, W. W. Norton & Company, New York, 1976, p. 144.

22 R. Ewing, P. Haliyur, and G.W. Page, "Getting Around a Traditional City, a Suburban PUD, and Everything In-Between," *Transportation Research Record 1466*, 1994, pp. 53-62; and R. Ewing, "Beyond Density, Mode Choice, and Single-Purpose Trips," *Transportation Quarterly*, Vol. 49, Fall 1995, pp. 15-24.

23 Anti-sprawl provisions of Florida's Local Government Comprehensive Planning Rule are contained in 9J-5.006(5), Florida Administrative Code.

24 Real Estate Research Corporation, *The Costs of Sprawl: Environmental and Economic Costs of Alternative Residential Development Patterns at the Urban Fringe*, Council on Environmental Quality, Washington, D.C., 1974, p. 135; J.B. Schneider and J.R. Beck, "Reducing the Travel Requirements of the American City: An Investigation of Alternative Urban Spatial Structures," *Transportation Research Record 499*, 1974, pp. 12-30; J.S. Roberts, "Energy and Land Use: Analysis of Alternative Development Patterns," *Environmental Comment*, September 1975, pp. 2-11; Middlesex Somerset Mercer Regional Council, *The Impact of Various Land Use Strategies on Suburban Mobility: Final Report*, Princeton, N.J., 1991, pp. 53 and 57; R.J. Czerniak and P. DeCorla-Souza, "Toledo, Ohio: Alternative Transportation and Land Use Structures," *ITE 1992 Compendium of Technical Papers*, 1992, pp. 330-335; and P. Naess, "Can Urban Development Be Made Environmentally Sound?" *Journal of Environmental Planning and Management*, Vol. 36, 1993, pp. 309-333.

25 Florida's population is projected to grow by 39 percent between 1990 and 2010. Assuming constant household size, 28 percent of the residential development on the ground in 2010 will have been built during the 20-year period. If this increment of development generates half the vehicular travel per capita of Florida's current sprawl pattern, regional VMT will be about 14 percent lower with compact development than with continued sprawl. While crude, this calculation is not out of line with the results of a few fairly sophisticated urban form studies. See R. Ewing, "Characteristics, Causes, and Effects of Sprawl: A Literature Review," *Environmental and Urban Issues*, Vol. 21, Winter 1994, pp. 1-15.

26 W. Kulash, "Neotraditional Town Design: Will the Traffic Work?" Session Notes, AICP Workshop on Neotraditional Town Planning, American Institute of Certified Planners, Washington, D.C., 1991.

27 H.S. Levinson and K.R. Roberts, "System Configurations in Urban Transportation Planning, *Highway Research Record 64*, 1963, pp. 71-83; R.B. Peiser, "Land Use versus Road Network Design in Community Transport Cost Evaluation," *Land Economics*, Vol. 60, 1984, pp. 95-109; F.A. Curtis, L. Neilsen, and A. Bjornsor, "Impact of Residential Street Design on Fuel Consumption," *Journal of Urban Planning and Development*, Vol. 110, 1984, pp. 1-8; and M.G. McNally and S. Ryan, "Comparative Assessment of Travel Characteristics for Neotraditional Designs," *Transportation Research Record 1400*, 1993, pp. 67-77.

28 See Snohomish County Transportation Authority, *A Guide to Land Use and Public Transportation*, Technology Sharing Progam, U.S. Department of Transportation, Washington, D.C., 1989, pp. 7-6 and 7-7; C. Stapleton, *Planning and Road Design for New Residential Sub-Divisions: Guidelines*, Director General of Transport for South Australia, Adelaide, 1988, p. 29; Model Code Task Force, *Australian Model Code for Residential Development*, Department of Health, Housing and Community Services, Commonwealth of Australia, Canberra, 1990, pp. 48-51; Main Roads Department, *Guidelines for Local Area Traffic Management*, East Perth, Western Australia, 1990, p. 92; W. Bowes, M. Gravel, and G. Noxon, *Guide to Transit Considerations in the Subdivision Design and Approval Process*, Transportation Association of Canada, Ottawa, Ontario, 1991, p. A-8; Department of Planning and Housing, *Victorian Code for Residential Development: Subdivision and Single Dwellings*, State Government of Victoria, Melbourne, Australia, 1992, pp. 37-41; Ontario Ministry of Transportation, *Transit-Supportive Land Use Planning Guidelines*, Toronto, 1992, pp. 45-46; and Denver Regional Council of Governments, *Suburban Mobility Design Manual*, Denver, 1993, p. 26.

29 A. Duany and E. Plater-Zyberk, "The Second Coming of the American Small Town," *Wilson Quarterly*, Vol. 16, 1992, pp. 19-48.

30 American Institute of Architects, op. cit., p. 7. Some urban designers might object to this characterization as too limiting. Indeed, the best-known designers are famous for their pronoucements on urban form, community layout, and street network structure. However, when they address such issues, they have crossed over the line between design and planning to become leading practitioners in another field. The traditional concerns of urban design are small-scale and aesthetic (where "aesthetic" is defined broadly to include neighborhood identity, vibrant street life, etc.).

See, for example, E.N. Bacon, *Design of Cities*, Viking Press, New York, 1974; R. Hedman, *Fundamentals of Urban Design*, American Planning Association, Chicago, 1984; C. Alexander et al., *A New Theory of Urban Design*, Oxford University Press, New York, 1987; and K. Lynch, "Urban Design," in T. Banerjee and M. Southworth (eds.), *City Sense and City Design: Writing and Projects of Kevin Lynch*, MIT Press, Cambridge, Mass., 1990, pp. 580-617.

31 S.L. Handy, "Regional Versus Local Accessibility: Implications for Non-Work Travel," *Transportation Research Record 1400*, 1993, pp. 58-66; R. Cervero, "Evidence on Travel Behavior in Transit-Supportive Residential Neighborhoods," *Transit-Supportive Development in the United States: Experiences and Prospects*, Technology Sharing Program, U.S. Department of Transportation, Washington, D.C., 1993, pp. 127-163; Parsons Brinckerhoff Quade Douglas, Inc., *The Pedestrian Environment*, 1000 Friends of Oregon, Portland, 1993, pp. 29-34; Sasaki Associates, Inc., *Transit and Pedestrian Oriented Neighborhoods*, Maryland-National Capital Park & Planning Commission, Silver Spring, 1993, pp. 47-53; R. Cervero and R. Gorham, "Commuting in Transit Versus Automobile Neighborhoods," *Journal of the American Planning Association*, Vol. 61, 1995, pp. 210-225; Cambridge Systematics, Inc., *The Effects of Land Use and Travel Demand Management Strategies on Commuting Behavior*, Technology Sharing Program, U.S. Department of Transportation, Washington, D.C., 1994a, pp. 3-19 through 3-21; B. Friedman, S.P. Gordon, and J.B. Peers, "Effect of Neotraditional Neighborhood Design on Travel Characteristics," *Transportation Research Record 1466*, 1994, pp. 63-70; S.L. Handy, "Understanding The Link Between Urban Form and Travel Behavior," paper presented at the 74th Annual Meeting, Washington, D.C., 1995; A. Kulkarni, R. Wang, and M.G. McNally, "Variation of Travel Behavior in Alternative Network and Land Use Structures," *ITE 1995 Compendium of Technical Papers*, Institute of Transportation Engineers, Washington, D.C., 1995, pp. 372-375; and S. Handy, "Urban Form and Pedestrian Choices: Study of Austin Neighborhoods," *Transportation Research Record 1552*, 1996, pp. 135-144.

32 Duany and Plater-Zyberk, op. cit.; P. Langdon, "A Good Place to Live," *The Atlantic Monthly*, Vol. 261, March 1988, pp. 39-60; A. Duany and E. Plater-Zyberk, *Towns and Town-Making Principles*, Rizzoli International Publications, New York, 1991; D. Mohney and K. Easterling (eds.), *Seaside: Making a Town in America*, Princeton Architectural Press, New York, 1991; L.W. Bookout, "Neotraditional Town Planning: A New Vision for the Suburbs?" *Urban Land*, Vol. 51, January 1992, pp. 20-26; and P. Katz, "Seaside," *The New Urbanism: Toward an Architecture of Community*, McGraw-Hill, New York, 1994, pp. 2-17.

33 The designer is Peter Calthorpe, and he cites Mizner Park in his talks though not

yet in his writings. P. Calthorpe, "Pedestrian Pockets: New Strategies for Suburban Growth," in D. Kelbaugh (ed.), *The Pedestrian Pocket Book: A New Suburban Design Strategy*, Princeton Architectural Press, New York, 1989, pp. 7-20; and P. Calthorpe, *The Next American Metropolis: Ecology, Community and the American Dream*, Princeton Architectural Press, New York, 1993. For more on the subject of urban and urbane centers in the suburbs, see P. Langdon, "Pumping Up Suburban Downtowns," *Planning*, Vol. 56, July 1990, pp. 22-28; J.H. Kay, "Building a *There* There," *Planning*, Vol. 57, January 1991, pp. 4-8; and J.R. Molinaro, "Creating a Vibrant Urban Core in the Suburbs," *Land Development*, Vol. 5, Winter 1993, pp. 16-20.

34 Hedman and Jaszeski, op. cit., pp. 82-102; R.F. Galehouse, "Mixed-Use Centers in Suburban Office Parks," *Urban Land*, Vol. 43, August 1984, pp. 10-13; R.K. Untermann, "Adapting Suburban Communities," *Accommodating the Pedestrian: Adapting Towns and Neighborhoods for Walking and Bicycling*, Van Nostrand Reinhold Co., New York, 1984, pp. 173-229; R.E. Knack, "Zipping Up the Strip," *Planning*, Vol. 52, July 1986, pp. 22-27; T. Fisher, "Remaking Malls," *Progressive Architecture*, Vol. 69, November 1988, pp. 96-101; R. Hedman, "Suburban Sketchbook," *Planning*, Vol. 55, December 1989, pp. 16-17; K. Lynch and M. Southworth, "Designing and Managing the Strip," in T. Banerjee and M. Southworth (eds.), *City Sense and City Design: Writing and Projects of Kevin Lynch*, MIT Press, Cambridge, Mass., 1990, pp. 580-617; R.K. Untermann, "New Design Strategies for the Entire Road," *Linking Land Use and Transportation: Design Strategies to Serve HOVs and Pedestrians*, Washington State Department of Transportation, Seattle, 1991, Section 2; R.E. Knack, "Park and Shop: Some Guidelines," *Planning*, Vol. 58, May 1992, pp. 18-23; A. Achimore, "Putting the Community Back into Community Retail," *Urban Land*, Vol. 52, August 1993, pp. 33-38; S. DeSantis, T. Kirk, and D. Arambula, *1993 Land Use, Transportation and Air Quality: A Manual for Planning Practitioners*, The Planning Center, Newport Beach, Calif., 1993; Snohomish County Transportation Authority, *A Guide to Land Use and Public Transportation - Volume II: Applying the Concepts*, Lynnwood, Wash., 1993, Chapters 3-5 ("Transit-Compatible Site Plans," "Transit-Friendly Shopping Centers," and "Redesign of a Strip Commercial Area"); D. Schwanke, T.J. Lassar, and M. Beyard, *Remaking the Shopping Center*, Urban Land Institute, Washington, D.C., 1994, pp. 31-89; I.F. Thomas, "Reinventing the Regional Mall," *Urban Land*, Vol. 53, February 1994, pp. 24-27; T. Lassar, "Shopping Centers *Can* Be Good Neighbors, *Planning*, Vol. 61, October 1995, pp. 14-19; W. Fulton, "Are Edge Cities Losing Their Edge?" *Planning*, Vol. 62, May 1996, pp. 4-7; and I.F. Thomas, "New Thinking on Regional Shopping Centers," *Urban Land*, Vol. 55, May 1996, pp. 24-27, 57.

35 Downs, op. cit., 1992, p. 34.

36 Institute of Transportation Engineers (ITE), *A Toolbox for Alleviating Traffic Congestion*, Washington, D.C., 1989.

37 Alan M. Voorhees and Associates, "Guidelines to Reduce Energy Consumption through Transportation Actions," in *Energy Primer: Selected Transportation Topics*, Technology Sharing Program, U.S. Department of Transportation, Washington, D.C., 1975, pp. 58-75; F.A. Wagner, *Traffic Control System Improvements: Impacts and Costs*, Federal Highway Administration, Washington, D.C., 1980; Barton-Aschman Associates, *Traveler's Response to Transportation System Changes*, Federal Highway Administration, Washington, D.C., 1981; F.A. Wagner, "Energy Impacts of Urban Transportation Improvements," in H.S. Levinson and R.A. Weant (eds.), *Urban Transportation: Perspectives and Prospects*, Eno Transportation Foundation, Landsdowne, Va., 1982, pp. 168-176; H.S. Levinson, M. Golenberg, and K. Zografos, "Transportation System Management: How Effective? Some Perspectives on Benefits and Impacts," *Transportation Research Record 1142*, 1987, pp. 22-32; W.R. Loudon and D.A. Dagang, "Predicting the Impact of Transportation Control Measures on Travel Behavior and Pollutant Emissions," paper presented at the 71st Annual Meeting, Transportation Research Board, Washington, D.C., 1992; D.A. Dagang, "Transportation Demand Management Cost-Effectiveness Model for Suburban Employers," *Transportation Research Record 1404*, 1993, pp. 64-72; L.O. Pehlke, "New Modeling Techniques for Evaluation of Transportation Control Measures and Congestion Management Techniques," in J.M. Faris (ed.), *Fourth National Conference on Transportation Planning Methods Applications—Volume I*, Transportation Research Board, Washington, D.C., 1993, pp. 287-304; Apogee Research, Inc., *Costs and Effectiveness of Transportation Control Measures (TCMs): A Review and Analysis of the Literature*, National Association of Regional Councils, Washington, D.C., 1994. and D.L. Schrank and T.J. Lomax, "Estimating the Effect of Operational Improvements in the Houston Area," *Tranportation Research Record 1564*, 1996, pp. 30-39.

38 P. DeCorla-Souza and R. Schoeneberg, "The Transportation-Air Quality Connection: Perceptions and Realities," *ITE 1992 Compendium of Technical Papers*, Institute of Transportation Engineers, Washington, D.C., 1992, pp. 157-162; C.K. Orski, "Employee Trip Reduction Programs: An Evaluation," *Transportation Quarterly*, Vol. 47, 1993, pp. 327-341; and ITE Technical Council Committee 6Y-51, *Evaluation of Employee Trip Reduction Programs Based on California's Experience with Regulation XV*, Institute of Transportation Engineers, Washington, D.C., 1994.

39 W. Owen, *The Accessible City*, The Brookings Institution, Washington, D.C., 1972, p. 56.

40 Studies relating home-based travel patterns to residential accessibility include: Ewing et al., op. cit.; Ewing, op. cit., 1995; Handy, op. cit., 1992; Handy, op. cit., 1993; Handy, op. cit., 1995; Handy, op. cit., 1996; Parsons Brinckerhoff Quade Douglas, op. cit., pp. 29-34; S. Hanson, "The Determinants of Daily Travel-Activity Patterns: Relative Location and Sociodemographic Factors," *Urban Geography*, Vol. 3, 1982, pp. 179-202; S. Hanson and M. Schwab, "Accessibility and Intraurban Travel," *Environment and Planning A*, Vol. 19, 1987, pp. 735-748; P.A. Williams, "A Recursive Model of Intraurban Trip-Making," *Environment and Planning A*, 1988, Vol. 20, pp. 535-546; P.A. Williams, "The Influence of Residential Accessibility on Household Trip-Making," *Socio-Economic Planning Sciences*, Vol. 23, 1989, pp. 373-385; S. Tarry, "Accessibility Factors at the Neighborhood Level," in *Environmental Issues*, PTRC Education and Research Services Ltd., London, England, 1992, pp. 257-270; R. Kitamura, P.L. Mokhtarian, and L. Laidet, "A Micro-Analysis of Land Use and Travel in Five Neighborhoods in the San Francisco Bay Area," paper presented at the 74th Annual Meeting, Transportation Research Board, Washington, D.C., 1995; R. Cervero, "Mixed Land-Uses and Commuting: Evidence from the American Housing Survey," *Transportation Research A*, Vol. 30, 1996a, pp. 361-377; R. Cervero and K. Kockelman "Travel Demand and the 3Ds: Density, Diversity, and Design," paper submitted to *Transportation Research D*, 1996; and C.L. Purvis, M. Iglesias, and V. Eisen, "Incorporating Work Trip Accessibility in Nonwork Trip Generation Models in the San Francisco Bay Area," paper presented at the 75th Annual Meeting, Transportation Research Board, Washington, D.C., 1996.

41 Ewing et al., op. cit.; Ewing, op. cit., 1995; S. Hanson, op. cit.; Hanson and Schwab, op. cit.; and Williams, op. cit., 1988.

42 A.J. Richardson and W. Young, "A Measure of Linked-Trip Accessibility," *Transportation Planning and Technology*, Vol. 7, 1982, pp. 73-82.

43 The merits of different urban forms have been hotly debated. We attempt in our discussion to make sense out of the often-contradictory literature. See, in particular, P. Gordon and H. Richardson, "Are Compact Cities a Desirable Planning Goal?" *Journal of the American Planning Association*, Vol. 63, 1997, pp. 95-106; and R. Ewing, "Is Los Angeles-Style Sprawl Desirable?" *Journal of the American Planning Association*, Vol. 63, 1997, pp. 107-126. Also see P. Gordon, A. Kumar, and H.W. Richardson, "The Influence of Metropolitan Spatial Structure on Commuting Time," *Journal of Urban Economics*, Vol. 26, 1989, pp. 138-151; G. Giuliano, "Research Policy and Review 27. New Directions for Understanding Transportation and Land Use," *Environment and Planning A*, Vol. 21, 1989, pp. 145-159; P.W.G. Newman and J.R. Kenworthy, "Gasoline Consumption and Cities: A Comparison of U.S. Cities with a Global Survey," *Journal of the American Planning Association*, Vol. 55, 1989, pp. 24-37; P. Gordon and H.W. Richardson, "Gasoline Consumption and Cities: A Reply," *Journal of the American Planning Association*, Vol. 55, 1989, pp. 342-346; P. Gordon, H.W. Richardson, and M. Jun, "The Commuting Paradox: Evidence from the Top Twenty," *Journal of the American Planning Association*, Vol. 57, 1991, pp. 416-420; R.L. Morrill, "Myths about Metropolis," in J.F. Hart (ed.), *Our Changing Cities*, Johns Hopkins Press, Baltimore, 1991, pp. 1-11; P.W.G. Newman and J.R. Kenworthy, *Cities and Automobile Dependence: A Sourcebook*, Gower Technical, Brookfield, Vt., 1991, pp. 34-68; L.S. Bourne, "Self-Fulfilling Prophecies? Decentralization, Inner City Decline, and the Quality of Urban Life," *Journal of the American Planning Association*, Vol. 58, 1992, pp. 509-513; A. Downs, *Stuck in Traffic: Coping with Peak-Hour Congestion*, The Brookings Institution, Washington, D.C., 1992, pp. 79-97, 112-120; P.W.G. Newman and J.R. Kenworthy, "Is There A Role for Physical Planners," *Journal of the American Planning Association*, Vol. 58, 1992, pp. 353-362; M. Wachs, "The Role of Land Use Strategies for Improving Transportation and Air Quality," Introductory remarks to the UCLA Extension Public Policy Program Symposium on the Transportation/Land Use/Air Quality Connection, Lake Arrowhead, Calif., 1993; A. Downs, *New Visions for Metropolitan America*, The Brookings Institution, Washington, D.C., 1994, pp. 123-165; P. Gordon and H.W. Richardson, "Sustainable Congestion," in J. Brothchie et al. (eds.), *Cities in Competition: Productive and Sustainable Cities for the 21st Century*, Longman Australia, Melbourne, Australia, 1994, pp. 348-58; W.P. Anderson, P.S. Kanaroglou, and E.J. Miller, "Urban Form, Energy and the Environment: A Review of Issues, Evidence and Policy," *Urban Studies*, Vol. 33, pp. 7-35; and P. Gordon and H.W. Richardson, "Beyond Polycentricity: The Dispersed Metropolis, Los Angeles, 1970-1990," *Journal of the American Planning Association*, Vol. 62, 1996, pp. 289-95. The equally contradictory European literature is reviewed in M.J. Breheny, "The Contradictions of the Compact City: A Review," in M.J. Breheny (ed.), *Sustainable Development and Urban Form*, Pion Limited, London, 1992, pp. 138-159; and D. McLaren, "Compact or Dispersed? Dilution Is No Solution," *Built Environment*, Vol. 18, 1992, pp. 268-284. The related debate over the merits of jobs-housing balance is aired in: Downs, op. cit., 1992, pp. 98-111; R. Cervero, "Jobs-Housing Balancing and Regional Mobility," *Journal of the American Planning Association*, Vol. 55, 1989, pp. 136-150; L.W. Bookout, "Jobs and Housing: The Search for Balance," *Urban Land*, Vol. 49, October 1990, pp. 5-9; G. Giuliano, "Is Jobs-Housing Balance a Transportation Issue?" *Transportation Research Record 1305*, 1991, pp. 305-312; D.M. Nowlan and G. Stewart, "Downtown Population Growth and Commuting Trips: Recent Experience in Toronto," *Journal of the American Planning Association*, Vol. 57, 1991, pp. 165-182; San Diego Association of Governments, "Jobs/Housing Balance and Transportation Corridor Densities," Appendix 3 of *Regional Growth Management Strategy*, San Diego, 1991; A. Sherwood, "Jobs-Housing

Balance," in *Achieving a Jobs-Housing Balance: Land Use Planning for Regional Growth*, Resource Manual, Lincoln Institute of Land Policy, Cambridge, Mass., 1991; M. Wachs, "Thought Piece on the Jobs/Housing Balance," in *Achieving a Jobs-Housing Balance: Land Use Planning for Regional Growth*, Resource Manual, Lincoln Institute of Land Policy, Cambridge, Mass., 1991; J.C. Levine, "Decentralization of Jobs and the Emerging Suburban Commute," *Transportation Research Record 1364*, 1992, pp. 71-80; R. Cervero, "Community Development, Land Use Patterns, and Commuting Choices," *Transit-Supportive Development in the United States: Experiences and Prospects*, Technology Sharing Program, U.S. Department of Transportation, Washington, D.C., 1993, pp. 164-216; G. Giuliano and K. Small, "Is the Journey to Work Explained by Urban Structure?" *Urban Studies*, Vol. 30, 1993, pp. 1485-1500; M. Wachs et al., "The Changing Commute: A Case-Study of the Jobs-Housing Relationship over Time," *Urban Studies*, Vol. 30, 1993, pp. 1711-1729; L.D. Frank and G. Pivo, *Relationships Between Land Use and Travel Behavior in the Puget Sound Region*, Washington State Department of Transportation, Seattle, 1994, pp. 30-34; R. Ewing, *Best Development Practices: Doing the Right Thing and Making Money at the Same Time*, American Planning Association, Chicago, 1996a, p. 19; and R. Cervero, "Jobs-Housing Balance Revisited: Trends and Impacts in the San Francisco Bay Area," *Journal of the American Planning Association*, Vol. 62, 1996b, pp. 492-510.

44 Studies reaching this conclusion, including John Holtzclaw's own, are summarized in J. Holtzclaw, *Explaining Urban Density and Transit Impacts on Auto Use*, Sierra Club, San Francisco, 1991, pp. 25 and 34-58; and J. Holtzclaw, *Using Residential Patterns and Transit to Decrease Auto Dependence and Costs*, Natural Resources Defense Council, San Francisco, 1994, pp. 6-8 and 20-21. Also see Cervero, op. cit., 1996a; Cervero and Kockelman, op. cit.; Frank and Pivo, op. cit., pp. 14-34; Kitamura et al., op. cit.; Parsons Brinckerhoff Quade Douglas, op. cit.; H.S. Levinson and F.H. Wynn, "Effects of Density on Urban Transportation Requirements," *Highway Research Record 2*, 1963, pp. 38-64; J.B. Lansing and E. Mueller, "Residential Location and Urban Mobility," *Highway Research Record 106*, 1966, pp. 77-76; Wilbur Smith and Associates, *Patterns of Car Ownership, Trip Generation and Trip Sharing in Urbanized Areas*, U.S. Department of Transportation, Washington, D.C., 1968, pp. 107-110; K. Neels et al., *An Empirical Investigation of the Effects of Land Use on Urban Travel*, The Urban Institute, Washington, D.C., 1977, pp. 8-34, 56-67; D.T. Hunt et al., "A Geodemographic Model for Bus Service Planning and Marketing," *Transportation Research Record 1051*, 1986, pp. 1-12; G. Harvey, *Relation of Residential Density to VMT Per Resident*, Metropolitan Transportation Commission, Oakland, 1990; R.J. Spillar and G.S. Rutherford, "The Effects of Population Density and Income on Per Capita Transit Ridership in Western American Cities," *ITE 1990 Compendium of Technical Papers*, Institute of Transportation Engineers, Washington, D.C., 1990, pp. 327-331; P.D. Prevedouros, "Trip Generation: Different Rates for Different Densities," paper presented at the 71st Annual Meeting of the Transportation Research Board, Washington, D.C., 1991; K.M. Kockelman, "Which Matters More in Mode Choice: Density or Income?" *ITE 1995 Compendium of Technical Papers*, Institute of Transportation Engineers, Washington, D.C., 1995, pp. 844-867; R.T. Dunphy and K.M. Fisher, "Transportation, Congestion, and Density: New Insights," *Transportation Research Record 1552*, 1996, pp. 89-96; T. Messinger and R. Ewing, "Transit-Oriented Development in the Sunbelt," *Transportation Research Record 1552*, 1996, pp. 145-152; and P. Schimek, "Household Vehicle Ownership and Use: How Much Does Residential Density Matter?" *Transportation Research Record 1552*, 1996, pp. 120-125.

45 Studies comparing centralized development to low-density sprawl consistently find the former to be more energy-efficient (reflecting reduced travel requirements). But when multicentered development is added to the mix, it emerges as the preferred alternative from an energy-efficiency standpoint. See the literature review in V.A. Haines, "Energy and Urban Form: A Human Ecological Critique," *Urban Affairs Quarterly*, Vol. 21, 1986, pp. 337-353.

46 Middlesex Somerset Mercer Regional Council, op. cit.; San Diego Association of Governments, op. cit.; North Central Texas Council of Governments, *Urban Form/Transportation System Options for the Future: Dallas/Fort Worth Case Study*, Arlington, 1990; Puget Sound Council of Governments, *Summary and Comparison Between Alternatives*, Vision 2020, Seattle, 1990; Metropolitan Washington Council of Governments, *Transportation Demand Impacts of Alternative Land Use Scenarios, Final Report*, Washington, D.C., 1991; Baltimore Regional Council of Governments, *Impact of Land Use Alternatives on Transportation Demand*, Baltimore, 1992; Cambridge Systematics, Inc., *The LUTRAQ Alternative/Analysis of Alternatives: An Interim Report*, 1000 Friends of Oregon, Portland, 1992; G.V. Wickstrom and R.J. Milone, "Transportation Demand Impacts of Alternative Land Use Scenarios," in J.M. Faris (ed.), *Fourth National Conference on Transportation Planning Methods Applications—Volume I*, Transportation Research Board, Washington, D.C., 1993, pp. 65-93; Chesapeake Bay Foundation, *A Network of Livable Communities: Evaluating Travel Behavior Effects of Alternative Transportation and Community Designs for the National Capital Region*, Annapolis, MD, 1996; and T.A. Steiss, "Testing the Impact of Alternative Land Use Scenarios Using a Travel Forecasting Model," paper presented at the 75th Annual Meeting, Transportation Research Board, Washington, D.C., 1996.

47 R.G. Schiffer, "Developing Long Range Transportation Plans for Small Urbanized Areas in the ISTEA Era: The Tallahassee 2020 Plan Update," paper prepared for the

Fifth Conference on Transportation Planning Methods, available from the author at Post, Buckley, Schuh and Jernigan, Tallahassee, Fla., 1995.

48 Put another way, residents are more likely to patronize a nearby grocery store than a nearby furniture store, price and quality being more important than accessibility when it comes to big-ticket items like furniture. Also, residents make tens or hundreds of trips to grocery stores for every trip to a furniture store. Thus, from a travel standpoint, we gain much more by "internalizing" grocery stores within communities.

49 R. Ewing, *Developing Successful New Communities*, Urban Land Institute, Washington, D.C., 1991, pp. 74-87.

50 G. Herbert, "The Neighborhood Unit Principle and Organic Theory," *The Sociological Review*, Vol. 11, 1963, pp. 165-213; C. Alexander, "A City Is Not a Tree," *Design*, Vol. 46, 1966, pp. 46-55; S. Keller, "The Neighborhood Unit Reconsidered," *The Urban Neighborhood: A Sociological Perspective*, Random House, New York, 1968, pp. 125-147; T. Banerjee and W.C. Baer, *Beyond the Neighborhood Unit: Residential Environments and Public Policy*, Plenum Press, New York, 1984, pp. 187-190; K. Lynch and G. Hack, *Site Planning*, MIT Press, Cambridge, Mass., 1984, pp. 291-293; and B. Hillier, "Against Enclosure," in N. Teymur, T.A. Markus, and T. Woolley (eds.), *Rehumanizing Housing*, Butterworths, London, 1988, pp. 63-88.

51 Kulash, op. cit.; McNally and Ryan, op. cit.; J.R. Stone and C.A. Johnson, "Neo-Traditional Neighborhoods: A Solution to Traffic Congestion?" in R. E. Paaswell et al. (eds.), *Proceedings of the Site Impact Assessment Conference*, American Society of Civil Engineers, Washington, D.C., 1992. For studies of actual travel patterns versus land use mix, see Cambridge Systematics, op. cit., 1994a; Cervero, op. cit., 1996a; Cervero and Kockelman, op. cit.; Ewing, op. cit., 1995; Ewing et al., op. cit., 1994; Frank and Pivo, op. cit.; Handy, op. cit., 1992; Handy, op. cit., 1993; Handy, op. cit., 1995; and Handy, op. cit., 1996.; and Kitamura et al., op. cit.

52 Ewing et al., op. cit.

53 Ewing, 1996a, pp. 38-41.

54 From the literature, we have detailed information on work-related tours in several large suburban activity centers, a suburban downtown (Bellevue, Washington), an employment-rich suburb (Brentwood, Tennessee), and an urban downtown (Colorado Springs). See K.G. Hooper, *Travel Characteristics at Large-Scale Suburban Activity Centers*, National Cooperative Highway Research Program Report 323, Transportation Research Board, Washington, D.C., 1989, pp. 73-75, 86-93; D. Davidson, "The Impact of Suburban Employee Trip Chaining on Transportation Demand Management," *Transportation Research Record 1321*, 1991, pp. 82-89; F. Spielberg and A.T. Stoddard, "What Did You Do for Lunch Today? Midday Activities of Downtown Workers," *Transportation Research Record 1349*, 1992, pp. 115-117; and D. Davidson, "Role of Site Amenities as Transportation Demand Management Measures," *Transportation Research Record 1496*, 1995, pp. 184-190. A downtown Orlando commuter survey confirms the importance of grocery shopping, banking, dry cleaning, and day care services on the way to and from work. Downtown Orlando Transportation Management Association, *Survey Results: Commuting in Downtown Orlando*, 1991, p. 13.

55 Colorado/Wyoming Section Technical Committee, "Trip Generation for Mixed-Use Developments," *ITE Journal*, Vol. 57, 1987, pp. 27-32.

56 Davidson, op. cit., 1995.

57 Typical of these surveys is one that asked employees of Irvine Business Complex outside Los Angeles: "What prevents you from using a bus, carpool, or vanpool? (Check all that apply.)" Thirty percent of respondents checked "run other errands en route;" 13 percent checked "drop off child en route." L.J. Glazer and D.A. Curry, "A Ridesharing Market Analysis Survey of Commuter Attitudes at a Major Suburban Employment Center," *Tranportation Research Record 1130*, 199, pp. 9-13.

58 R. Cervero, "Land Use Mixing and Suburban Mobility," *Transportation Quarterly*, Vol. 42, 1988, pp. 429-446; R. Cervero, *America's Suburban Centers: The Land Use-Transportation Link*, Unwin Hyman, Boston, 1989, pp. 134-142; and R. Cervero, "Land Use and Travel at Suburban Activity Centers," *Transportation Quarterly*, Vol. 45, 1991, pp. 479-491.

59 M. Wachs, "Policy Implications of Recent Behavioral Research in Transportation Demand Management," *Journal of Planning Literature*, Vol. 5, 1991, pp. 333-341.

60 E. Ferguson, C. Ross, and M. Meyer, *Transportation Management Associations in the United States*, Office of Technology Sharing, U.S. Department of Transportation, Washington, D.C., 1992; COMSIS Corporation et al., *Implementing Effective Travel Demand Management Measures: A Series on TDM*, Institute of Transportation Engineers, Washington, D.C., 1993; and EG&G/Dynatrend, *Transportation Implications of Telecommuting*, Office of the Secretary, U.S. Department of Transportation, Wash-

ington, D.C., 1993.

61 C.P. Flynn and L.J. Glazer, "Ten Cities' Strategies for Transportation Demand Management," *Transportation Research Record 1212*, 1989, pp. 11-23; KPMG Peat Marwick, *Status of Traffic Mitigation Ordinances*, Urban Mass Transportation Administration, Washington, D.C., 1989; E. Ferguson, "Transportation Demand Management: Planning, Development, and Implementation," *Journal of the American Planning Association*, Vol. 56, 1990, pp. 442-456; T.H. Higgins, "Guidelines for Developing Local Demand Management or Trip Reduction Policies," *Transportation Research Record 1280*, 1990, pp. 11-21; Center for Urban Transportation Research (CUTR), *Commute Alternatives Systems Handbook*, University of South Florida, Tampa, 1992, pp. 57-65; E. Sanford and E. Ferguson, "Overview of Trip Reduction Ordinances in the United States: The Vote Is Still Out on Their Effectiveness," *Transportation Research Record 1321*, 1991, pp. 135-137; E. Ferguson, C. Ross, and M. Meyer, "Transportation Management Associations: Organization, Implementation, and Evaluation," *Transportation Research Record 1346*, 1992, pp. 36-43; and R. Ewing, "TDM, Growth Management, and the Other Four Out of Five Trips, *Transportation Quarterly*, Vol. 47, 1993a, pp. 343-366.

62 Post, Buckley, Schuh & Jernigan, Inc., *A Transportation Demand Management Program: Final Report*, Tallahassee-Leon County Metropolitan Planning Organization, Tallahassee, Fla., 1994, pp. 5-1 through 5-11.

63 The Tallahassee experience illustrates a point about mandatory trip reduction programs: Whatever their merits from a transportation standpoint, they are not popular with employers, a powerful constituency. Several states and regions have suspended or relaxed employer-based programs due to concerns about equity. "Why should employers be forced to manage their employees' travel?" is a common refrain. Z.A. Farkas, "The Equity and Cost Effectiveness of Employee Commute Options," paper presented at the 75th Annual Meeting, Transportation Research Board, Washington, D.C., 1996.

64 The cost estimates were based on an Ernst & Young audit of Regulation XV, the trip reduction measure for the Los Angeles area. The base cost, $105 per employee, was used to generate alarming estimates of cost per vehicle trip eliminated.

65 E.N. Schreffler, "How Costly and Cost Effective Are ECO Programs?" *ITE 1996 Compendium of Technical Papers*, Institute of Transportation Engineers, Washington, D.C., 1996, pp. 384-388. Also see J. Stewart, "Evaluating the Cost-Effectiveness of Employer-Based Trip Reduction Programs: Reviewed and Reexamined," *Transportation Research Record 1433*, 1994, pp. 164-169.

66 Free parking is taxed only if it is valued at more than $155 per month, whereas subsidies for transit and vanpools become taxable at $60 per month.

67 Gruen Gruen + Associates, *Employment and Parking in Suburban Business Parks: A Pilot Study*, Urban Land Institute, Washington, D.C., 1986, pp. 13-15; D. Hitchcock, *Providing Transportation for Activity Centers*, Joint Center for Urban Mobility Research, Houston, 1987; H.S. Stein, "Parking Study of Neighborhood and Community Shopping Centers," *Transportation Research Record 1299*, 1991, pp. 19-27; Municipality of Metropolitan Seattle, *1991 Parking Utilization Study*, 1992; E. Kadesh and J. Peterson, "Parking Utilization at Worksites in King and South Snohomish Counties, Washington," *Transportation Research Record 1459*, 1994, p. 58-62; and R.W. Willson, "Suburban Parking Requirements: A Tacit Policy for Automobile Use and Sprawl," *Journal of the American Planning Association*, Vol. 61, 1995, pp. 29-42.

68 For case studies, see K. Bhatt and T. Higgins, *An Assessment of Travel Demand Management Approaches at Suburban Employment Centers*, Technology Sharing Program, U.S. Department of Transportation, Washington, D.C., 1989; COMSIS Corporation, *Evaluation of Travel Demand Management Measures to Relieve Congestion*, Technology Sharing Program, U.S. Department of Transportation, Washington, D.C., 1990; R. Dowling, D. Feltham, and W. Wycko, "Factors Affecting Transportation Demand Management Program Effectiveness at Six San Franscisco Medical Institutions," *Transportation Research Record 1321*, 1991, pp. 109-117; and G.S. Rutherford et al., "Transportation Demand Management: Case Studies of Medium-Sized Employers," *Transportation Research 1459*, 1994, pp. 7-16. For mode choice modeling results, see B.P. Feeney, "A Review of the Impact of Parking Policy Measures on Travel Demand," *Transportation Planning and Technology*, Vol. 13, 1989, pp. 229-244; R.W. Willson, "Estimating the Travel and Parking Demand Effects of Employer-Paid Parking," *Regional Science and Urban Economics*, Vol. 22, 1992, pp. 133-145; J. Morrall and D. Bolger, "The Relationship Between Downtown Parking Supply and Transit Use," *ITE Journal*, Vol. 66, 1996, pp. 32-36; and Z. Peng, K.J. Dueker, and J.G. Strathman, "Residential Location, Employment Location, and Commuter Responses to Parking Charges," *Transportation Research Record 1556*, 1996, pp. 109-118.

69 D.C. Shoup and R.W. Willson, "Employer-Paid Parking: The Problem and Proposed Solutions, *Transportation Quarterly*, Vol. 46, 1992, pp. 169-192.

70 D. Ehrlich, "Charging for Parking in Suburban Areas: Case Studies of Worksites

in King County," paper presented at the 75th Annual Meeting, Transportation Research Board, Washington, D.C., 1996.

71 D.C. Shoup, "Cashing Out Employer-Paid Parking: A Precedent for Congestion Pricing?" in *Curbing Gridlock: Peak-Period Fees to Relieve Traffic Congestion—Volume 2*, Special Report 242, Transportation Research Board, National Academy Press, Washington, D.C., 1994, pp. 152-199.

72 D. Shoup, *Evaluating the Effects of Cashing Out Employer-Paid Parking: Eight Case Studies*, Institute of Transportation Studies, University of California at Los Angeles, 1997, pp. 5-6.

73 *U.S. Climate Change Action Plan*, 1993, p. 21.

74 Our review of 10 planned unit development (PUD) ordinances from around the state uncovered no case of credit being given for shared parking. Another review, this one of parking regulations in Dade County's 28 localities, found eight jurisdictions silent on the subject of shared parking, 13 with additive parking requirements for mixed-use developments, and only six with language allowing some relaxation of parking requirements for mixed-use developments. J. Bradley, "Toward a Common Parking Policy: A Cross-Jurisdictional Matrix Comparison of Municipal Off-Street Parking Regulations in Metropolitan Dade County, Florida," *Transportation Research Record 1564*, 1996, pp. 40-45.

75 Barton-Aschman Associates, Inc., *Shared Parking*, Urban Land Institute, Washington, D.C., 1983; T.P. Smith, *Flexible Parking Requirements*, American Planning Association, Washington, D.C., 1983; S.J. TenHoor and S.A. Smith, *Model Parking Code Provisions to Encourage Ridesharing and Transit Use (including a Review of Experience)*, Federal Highway Administration, Washington, D.C., 1983; J.B. Goldstein et al., *Development Standards for Retail and Mixed Use Centers*, Institute of Urban Studies, University of Texas, Arlington, 1984; T.J. Higgins, "Parking Requirements for Transit-Oriented Developments," *Transportation Research Record 1404*, 1993, pp. 50-54; and Institute of Transportation Engineers (ITE), *Shared Parking Planning Guidelines*, Washington, D.C., 1995. Also see S.J. TenHoor and S.A. Smith, "Parking-Requirement Reduction Process for Ridesharing: Current Practices, Evolving Issues, and Future Directions," *Transportation Research Record 940*, 1983, pp. 44-51; T.J. Higgins, "Flexible Parking Requirements for Office Developments: New Support for Public Parking and Ridesharing," *Transportation*, Vol. 12, 1985, pp. 343-359; T.J. Higgins, "Parking Management and Traffic Mitigation in Six Cities: Implications for Local Policy," *Transportation Research Record 1232*, 1989, pp. 60-67; and F. Markowitz, M. Jones, and Hans W. Korve, "Shared Parking and Parking Management Strategies for Mixed-Use Projects," *ITE 1991 Compendium of Technical Papers*, Institute of Transportation Engineers, Washington, D.C., 1991, pp. 572-574.

76 A Florida survey found that 94 percent of commuters have free parking at their workplaces. R.E. Goldsmith and C.F. Hofacker, *Florida Commuter Attitudes: Survey Results*, Florida Institute for Marketing Alternative Transportation, Florida State University, Tallahassee, 1993, p. 16.

77 Cambridge Systematics, op. cit, 1994a, pp. 3-3 through 3-21.

78 Davidson, op. cit., 1995; A. Adiv, "The Structure of the Work-Trip Based on Analysis of Trip Diaries in the San Francisco Bay Area," in S. Carpenter and P. Jones (eds.), *Recent Advances in Travel Demand Analysis*, Gower, Ardershot, UK, 1983, pp. 117-136; and C.K. Orski, "Why Do Commuters Drive Alone?" *Environment: Changing Our Transportation Priorities*, Institute of Transportation Engineers, Washington, D.C., 1994, pp. 113-116.

79 Sanford and Ferguson, op. cit.; Bhatt and Higgins, op. cit., p. 27; and R. Cervero and B. Griesenbeck, "Factors Influencing Commuting Choices in Suburban Labor Markets: A Case Analysis of Pleasanton, California," *Transportation Research A*, Vol. 22A, 1988, pp. 151-161.

80 Ewing, op. cit., 1993a; H.M. Brunso and D.T. Hartgen, "Community-Based Ridesharing: An Overlooked Option," *Transportation Research Record 914*, 1983, pp. 26-33; Technical Advisory Group, *Guidelines for Local Air Districts Considering Transportation Control Measures Directed at Heavy-Duty Truck Operations*, California Air Resources Board, El Monte, 1990, pp. 15-27; Cambridge Systematics, Inc., "Vehicle Use Limitations/Restrictions," *Transportation Control Measure Information Documents*, U.S. Environmental Protection Agency, Ann Arbor, Mich., 1992; A.G. Hobeika et al., "Real-Time Diversion Strategies for Congested Urban Networks," *Proceedings of the 1992 Annual Meeting of IVHS America—Volume 2*, IVHS America, Washington, D.C., 1992, pp. 706-716; J.S. Niles and P.A. Toliver, "IVHS Technology for Improving Ridesharing," *Proceedings of the 1992 Annual Meeting of IVHS America—Volume 2*, IVHS America, Washington, D.C., 1992, pp. 537-547; C.E. Wallace and A.K. Kilpatrick, "IVHS Implications for Transportation Demand Management," *Proceedings of the 1993 Annual Meeting of IVHS America*, IVHS America, Washington, D.C., 1993, pp. 131-139; R.R. Kowshik et al., "Development of User Needs and Functional Requirements for a Real-Time Ridesharing System," paper presented at 73nd Annual Meeting, Transportation Research Board, 1994; S. Michalak et al., "Assessing

Users' Needs for Dynamic Ridesharing," *Transportation Research Record 1459*, 1994, pp. 32-38; G.W. Euler and H.D. Robinson (eds.), "Travel Demand Management," *National ITS Program Plan—Volume II*, ITS America, Washington, D.C., 1995, pp. 87-124; C.K. Orski, "Thinking Small: Applying ITS Technologies to TDM," *ITE Journal*, Vol. 65, December 1995, pp. 57-60; J.M. Golob and G. Giuliano, "Smart Traveler Automated Ridermatching Service Lessons Learned for Future ATIS Initiatives," *Transportation Research Record 1537*, 1996, pp. 23-29; and A. Polydoropoulou et al., "Modeling Revealed and Stated En-Route Travel Response to Advanced Traveler Information Systems," *Transportation Research Record 1537*, 1996, pp. 38-45. Recently, so much has been written about congestion pricing that it is difficult to know what to cite. For international experiences, see A.D. May, "Road Pricing: An International Perspective," *Transportation*, Vol. 19, 1992, pp. 313-333; and articles in "Session 29: Road and Trip Pricing Approaches," *ITE 1993 Compendium of Technical Papers*, Institute of Transportation Engineers, Washington, D.C., 1993, pp. 1-40. For the U.S. experience, see B. Arrillaga, "U.S. Experience with Congestion Pricing," *ITE Journal*, December 1993, pp. 39-43; and Federal Highway Administration (FHWA), *Report on the Congestion Pricing Pilot Program*, Report to Congress, Washington, D.C., 1996. For future prospects, see Committee for Study on Urban Transportation Congestion Pricing, op. cit.

81 V.W. Inman et al., "TravTek Trip and Network Efficiency Evaluation Findings," presentation at the 1994 IVHS America Annual Meeting, IVHS America, Washington, D.C., 1994.

82 The nomenclature of ITS is constantly changing, a reflection of how much R&D activity has been generated by federal funding. Some terms used in this primer—including "advanced traveler information systems"—are now apparently passe. We use them anyway, for they are more descriptive than what superceded them. The ITS literature is too vast to be adequately cited here, but for starters see the 500-plus abstracts in ITS America, *Intelligent Transportation: Realizing the Future*, Third World Congress on Intelligent Transportation Systems, Washington, D.C., 1996, pp. 1-312. Also see case studies and state-of-the-art reports available from the Intelligent Transportation Systems Joint Program Office, *Intelligent Transportation Systems Publications Catalog*, U.S. Department of Transportation, Washington, D.C., October 1996. Experience to date is summarized in Mitretek Systems, *Key Findings from the Intelligent Transportation Systems Program: What Have We Learned?* Federal Highway Administration, Washington, D.C., 1996.

83 D.W. Harwood, *Effective Utilization of Street Width on Urban Arterials*, National Cooperative Highway Research Program Report 330, Transportation Research Board, Washington, D.C., 1990, p. 2.

84 ITE District 6 Technical Committee, "A Survey of Transportation Demand Management Experience in the U.S.," *ITE 1989 Compendium of Technical Papers*, Institute of Transportation Engineers, Washington, D.C., 1989, pp. 529-535.

85 Harwood, op. cit., pp. 9-15 and Appendix A; and T.F. Humphrey, "Highways: Getting the Most Out of the Existing System," in *A Toolbox for Alleviating Traffic Congestion*, Institute of Transportation Engineers, Washington, D.C., 1989, pp. 33-72.

86 W.A. Frick, "The Effect of Major Physical Improvements on Capacity and Safety," *Traffic Engineering*, Vol. 39, December 1968, pp. 14-20; Roy Jorgensen Associates, *Cost and Safety Effectiveness of Highway Design Elements*, National Cooperative Highway Research Program Report 197, Transportation Research Board, Washington, D.C., 1978, pp. 77-80; V.G. Stover, S.C. Tignor, and M.J. Rosenbaum, "Access Control and Driveways," *Synthesis of Safety Research Related to Traffic Control and Roadway Elements—Volume 1*, Federal Highway Administration, Washington, D.C., 1982, pp. 4-2 through 4-10; D. Ismart, "Access Management: State of the Art," *Third National Conference on Transportation Planning Applications*, Transportation Research Board, Washington, D.C., 1991; G. Long, C. Gan, and B.S. Morrison, *Safety Impacts of Selected Median and Access Design Features*, Transportation Research Center, University of Florida, Gainesville, 1993, pp. 36-59; P.S. Parsonson, M.G. Waters, and J.S. Fincher, "Effect on Safety of Replacing an Arterial Two-Way Left-Turn Lane with a Raised Median," *Conference Proceedings of the First National Access Management Conference*, Federal Highway Administration, U.S. Department of Transportation, 1993, pp. 265-269; W.M. Bretherton, "Are Raised Medians Safer Than Two-Way Left-Turn Lanes?" *ITE Journal*, Vol. 64, December 1994, pp. 20-25; H.S. Levinson, "Access Management on Suburban Roads," *Transportation Quarterly*, Vol. 48, 1994, pp. 315-325; Committee on Access Management, "Driveway and Street Intersection Spacing," *Transportation Research Circular*, Number 456, March 1996, pp. 5-10; N.J. Garber and T.E. White, "Guidelines for Commercial Driveway Spacing on Urban and Suburban Arterial Roads," in *Compendium of the 2nd National Conference on Access Management*, Transportation Research Board, Washington, D.C., 1996, pp. 231-248; B.K. Lall, D. Huntington, and A. Eghtedari, "Access Management and Traffic Safety," in *Compendium of the 2nd National Conference on Access Management*, Transportation Research Board, Washington, D.C., 1996, pp. 249-268; and Florida Department of Transportation, *Access Management: An Important Traffic Management Strategy*, Tallahassee, undated.

87 Access management practices around the U.S. are reviewed in Committee on

Access Management, op. cit., pp. 26-40; and F.J. Koepke and H.S. Levinson, *Access Management Guidelines for Activity Centers*, National Cooperative Highway Research Program Report 348, Transportation Research Board, Washington, D.C., 1992, pp. 13-22.

88 Systems Planning Office, *Chapter 14-97: State Highway System Access Management Classification System and Standards*, Florida Department of Transportation, Tallahassee, 1990; and Florida Department of Transportation (FDOT), *Access Management on the State Highway System*, Tallahassee, undated, pp. 3-4.

89 K.M. Williams et al., *Model Land Development & Subdivision Regulations That Support Access Management for Florida Cities and Counties*, Florida Department of Transportation, Tallahassee, 1994. Also see K.M. Williams and J.R. Forester, *Land Development Regulations that Promote Access Management*, National Cooperative Research Program Synthesis of Highway Practice 233, Transportation Research Board, Washington, D.C., 1996.

90 D. Syrek, "Accident Rates at Intersections," *Traffic Engineering*, Vol. 25, pp. 312-316; G.M. Ebbecke and J.J. Schuster, "Areawide Impact of Traffic Control Devices," *Transportation Research Record 644*, 1977, pp. 54-57; H.H. Bissell and L.G. Neudorff, "Criteria for Removing Traffic Signals," *ITE 1980 Compendium of Technical Papers*, Institute of Transportation Engineers, Washington, D.C., 1980, pp. 56-66; W.M. Bretherton, "Signal Warrants: Are They Doing the Job?" *ITE 1991 Compendium of Technical Papers*, Institute of Transportation Engineers, Washington, D.C., 1991, pp. 163-167; and J.N. LaPlante and C.R. Kropidlowski, "Stop Sign Warrants: Time for Change," *ITE Journal*, Vol. 62, 1992, pp. 25-29. Also see literature on roundabouts referenced below.

91 H.S. Lum and W.R. Stockton, "STOP Sign Versus YIELD Sign," *Transportation Research Record 881*, 1982, pp. 29-33; H.W. McGee and M.R. Blankenship, *Guidelines for Converting Stop to Yield Control at Intersections*, National Cooperative Highway Research Program Report 320, Transportation Research Board, Washington, D.C., 1989, pp. 3-17; and K. Todd, "Should Yield Stop?" *ITE Journal*, Vol. 63, May 1993, pp. 36-41.

92 The criticism of America's "wide roads and narrow nodes" should not be taken as an endorsement of multilane intersections with multiphase signals; rather it is a plea for greater use of roundabouts. L. Ourston, "British Interchanges, Intersections, and Traffic Control Devices," *Westernite*, Vol. 25, September-October 1992, pp. 1-6.

93 K. Todd, "Modern Rotaries: A Transportation System Management Alternative," *Transportation Research Record 737*, 1979, pp. 61-72; S. Sabanayagam, "Capacity Analysis of Unsignalized Traffic Circles," *ITE 1990 Compendium of Technical Papers*, Institute of Transportation Engineers, Washington, D.C., 1990, pp. 298-302; M.J. Wallwork, "Roundabouts for the U.S.A.," *ITE 1991 Compendium of Technical Papers*, Institute of Transportation Engineers, Washington, D.C., 1991, pp. 608-611; W.F. Savage and K. Al-Sahili, "Traffic Circles: A Viable Form of Intersection Control?" *ITE Journal*, Vol. 64, September 1994, pp. 40-45; E.J. Myers, "Modern Roundabouts for Maryland," *ITE Journal*, Vol. 64, October 1994, pp. 18-22; and L. Ourston, "Nonconforming Traffic Circle Becomes Modern Roundabout," *ITE 1994 Compendium of Technical Papers*, Institute of Transportation Engineers, Washington, D.C., 1994, pp. 275-278.

94 British and Australian accident studies are reviewed in A. O'Brien and E. Richardson, "Use of Roundabouts in Australia," *ITE 1985 Compendium of Technical Papers*, Institute of Transportation Engineers, Washington, D.C., 1985, pp. 180-187. Several European studies are reviewed in L. Ourston, "A Synthesis of Roundabout Safety Research, with Recent Increases in Numbers of Roundabouts in a Few Countries," unpublished manuscript available from the author, Leif Ourston & Associates, Santa Barbara, Calif., 1993. Also see Myers, op. cit.; Savage and Al-Sahili, op. cit.; M.A. Rahman and T. Hicks, "A Critical Look at Roundabouts," *ITE 1994 Compendium of Technical Papers*, Institute of Transportation Engineers, Washington, D.C., 1994, pp. 260-264; C. Schoon and J.V. Minnen, "The Safety of Roundabouts in the Netherlands," *Traffic Engineering + Control*, Vol. 35, 1994, pp. 142-147; and A. Flannery and T.K. Datta, "Modern Roundabouts and Traffic Crash Experience in the United States," *Transportation Research Record 1553*, 1996, pp. 103-109.

95 The City of Gainesville priced two traffic control options—a roundabout vs. an upgraded traffic signal system—for the intersection of S.E. 4th Avenue and S.E. 7th Street. The roundabout had the edge in both capital and operating costs, and was chosen over the upgraded signal.

96 Florida Department of Transportation (FDOT), *Florida Roundabout Guide*, Tallahassee, 1996.

97 L. Ourston and P. Doctors, *Roundabout Design Guidelines*, California Department of Transportation, Sacramento, 1994; and State Highway Administration, *Roundabout Design Guidelines*, Maryland Department of Transportation, Annapolis, 1994.

98 Department of Transport, *The Geometric Design of Roundabouts*, Her Majesty's

Stationery Office, London, 1984; and Austroads, *Guide to Traffic Engineering Practice—Part 6: Roundabouts*, Sydney, Australia, 1993.

99 State-of-the-art signal timing is described in P.S. Parsonson, *Signal Timing Improvement Practices*, National Cooperative Highway Research Program Synthesis of Highway Practice 172, Transportation Research Board, Washington, D.C., 1992; and D.B. Fambro, S.R. Sunkari, and S.M. Sangineni, *Implementation Guidelines for Retiming* Infrastructure Features for ITS Deployment in Metropolitan Areas," unpublished working paper, Washington, D.C., 1995.

100 Some Florida successes are described in V.P. Poteat, "Traffic Signal Retiming: It Works!" In *Strategies to Alleviate Traffic Congestion*, Institute of Transportation Engineers, Washington, D.C., 1988, pp. 297-307; F.R. Aleman and T.M. Allen, "Metropolitan Orlando Area Computerized Signal System," *ITE Journal*, Vol. 60, June 1990, pp. 21-23; and J.W. Buckholz, "The 10 Major Pitfalls of Coordinated Signal Timing," *ITE Journal*, Vol. 63, August 1993, pp. 26-29. Signal timing optimation programs in Florida and seven other states are summarized in E.D. Arnold, *Signal Timing Optimization - A Review of State Programs*, Virginia Transportation Research Council, Charlottesville, 1988.

101 IVHS America, *Strategic Plan for Intelligent Vehicle-Highway Systems in the United States*, Washington, D.C., 1992, pp. III-9 to III-19. Also see U.S. Department of Transportation, *Implementation of the National Vehicle Highway Systems (IVHS) Program Plan*, Report to Congress, Washington, D.C., 1994; G.W. Euler and H.D. Robinson (eds.), "Deployment," *National ITS Program Plan - Volume I*, ITS America, Washington, D.C., 1995, pp. 79-105; and Federal Highway Administration (FHWA), "Core Infrastructure Features for ITS Deployment in Metropolitan Areas," Unpublished working paper, Washington, D.C., 1995.

102 MITRE Corporation, *Intelligent Transportation Infrastructure Benefits: Expected and Experienced*, Federal Highway Administration, Washington, D.C., 1996; and Mitretek Systems, *Review of ITS Benefits: Emerging Successes*, Federal Highway Administration, Washington, D.C., 1996.

103 While Britain and Australia have had traffic-adaptive signal control systems for decades, U.S. practice has languished somewhere between time-of-day and traffic-responsive control. See critical reviews by Santiago, Bowcott, and Tarnoff in *Traffic Management*, Engineering Foundation, New York, 1991, pp. 1-21, 35-51.

104 They continually adjust phase splits, offsets, and cycle lengths, all of which are fixed under time-of-day control and constrained to pre-set combinations under traffic-responsive control. J.L. Grubba et al., "Combining Real Time, Adaptive Traffic Control and Machine Vision Detection for Advanced Traffic Management Systems," *ITE 1993 Compendium of Technical Papers*, Institute of Transportation Engineers, Washington, D.C., 1993, pp. 298-302; J.A. Genovese, "SCOOT in the USA," *ITE 1994 Compendium of Technical Papers*, Institute of Transportation Engineers, Washington, D.C., 1994, pp. 369-373; and P.T. Martin and S.L.M. Hockaday, "SCOOT: An Update," *ITE Journal*, Vol. 65, January 1995, pp. 44-48.

105 For performance information, see J.Y.K. Luk, "Two Traffic-Responsive Area Traffic Control Methods: SCAT and SCOOT," *Traffic Engineering + Control*, Vol. 25, January 1984, pp. 14-17 and 22; P. Davies et al., *Assessment of Advanced Technologies for Relieving Urban Traffic Congestion*, National Cooperative Highway Research Program Report 340, Transportation Research Board, Washington, D.C., 1991, pp. 15-20; D.I. Robertson and R.D. Bretherton, "Optimizing Networks of Traffic Signals in Real Time: The SCOOT Method," *IEEE Transactions on Vehicular Technology*, Vol. 40, February 1991, pp. 11-15; A.M. Khan, "Technological Responses to Urban Traffic Congestion—Part Two: The Technology of Traffic Management," *The Journal of Urban Technology*, Vol. 1, 1992, pp. 29-46; Road Commission for Oakland County, *Preliminary Evaluation of the SCATS in the Fast-Trac IVHS System*, Beverly Hills, Mich., 1993; W.L. Kelman, J.C. Greenough, and B.Y. Quan, "The Metropolitan Toronto SCOOT Demonstration Project: A Preliminary Evaluation Report," paper presented at the 73th Annual Meeting, Transportation Research Board, Washington, D.C., 1994; K. Rochester-Tennyson, *SCATS Kirkwood Highway System*, Bureau of Traffic, Delaware Department of Transportation, Wilmington, 1996; and S. Skehan, "Adaptive Traffic Control System," *ITE 1996 Compendium of Technical Papers*, Institute of Transportation Engineers, 1996, pp. 203-207. Today's best systems are somewhat less "adaptive" than their name implies. They will eventually be replaced by systems that allow cycle lengths to vary from intersection to intersection and make signal settings responsive to conditions considerably upstream of intersections. See P.J. Tarnoff, "Advanced Traffic Control: A Look at the 90s," in *Traffic Management*, Engineering Foundation, New York, 1991, pp. 35-51.

106 J.A. Lindley, "Urban Freeway Congestion: Quantification of the Problem and Effectiveness of Potential Solutions," *ITE Journal*, Vol. 57, January 1987, pp. 27-32.

107 Several such projects are described in U.S. Department of Transportation, *Intelligent Vehicle Highway Systems Projects*, Washington, D.C., 1994, pp. 15, 73, 97, and 325. Coordinated control strategies are outlined in F.J. Pooran, R. Sumner, and H.C. Lieu, *Coordinated Operation of Ramp Metering and Adjacent Traffic Signal Control*

Systems: Final Report, Federal Highway Administration, Washington, D.C., 1992; and F.J. Pooran and H.C. Lieu, "Implementation of Operating Strategies for Integrated Freeway/Arterial Control Systems," *ITE 1994 Compendium of Technical Papers*, Institute of Transportation Engineers, Washington, D.C., 1994, pp. 364-368.

108 A recent status report on freeway ramp metering summarized the benefits: accident rate reductions of 24 to 50 percent; increased traffic flows of 17 to 25 percent; and increased mainline speeds of 16 to 62 percent. G. Piotrowicz and J. Robinson, *Ramp Metering Status in North America—1995 Update*, Technology Sharing Program, U.S. Department of Transportation, Washington, D.C., 1995, p. 26. Also see Institute of Transportation Engineers, op. cit., pp. 37-38; J.H. Banks, "Performance Measurement of a Metered Freeway System," *Transportation Research Record 1173*, 1988, pp. 30-32; L.J. Corcoran and G.A. Hickman, "Freeway Ramp Metering Effects in Denver," *ITE 1989 Compendium of Technical Papers*, Institute of Transportation Engineers, Washington, D.C., 1989, pp. 513-517; and J. Robinson and M. Doctor, *Ramp Metering Status in North America*, Technology Sharing Program, U.S. Department of Transportation, Washington, D.C., 1989, pp. 3-8.

109 In simulations, an integrated system cuts total travel delay by 10 to 17 percent, depending on the degree of coordination between local traffic signals and freeway ramp meters. F.J. Pooran et al., "Development of System Operating Strategies for Ramp Metering and Traffic Signal Coordination," paper presented at the 73rd Annual Meeting, Transportation Research Board, Washington, D.C., 1994.

110 R. Cervero, "Making Transit Work in the Suburbs," *Transportation Research Record 1451*, 1994, pp. 3-11.

111 R. Cervero, "Urban Transit in Canada: Integration and Innovation at Its Best," *Transportation Quarterly*, Vol. 40, 1986, pp. 293-316; W.D. Warren, "Impacts of Land Use on Mass Transit Development: A Comparison of Canberra and Springfield," *Transportation Quarterly*, Vol. 42, 1988, pp. 223-242; J. Pucher, "Public Transport Developments: Canada vs. the United States," *Transportation Quarterly*, Vol. 48, 1994, pp. 65-78; P. Schimek, "Automobile and Public Transit Use in the USA and Canada: A Comparison of Postwar Trends," paper presented at the 75th Annual Meeting, Transportation Research Board, Washington, D.C., 1996; and P. Newman, "Reducing Automobile Dependence," *Environment and Urbanization*, Vol. 8, 1996, pp. 67-92.

112 R. Cervero, "Case Studies of Transit-Supportive Development at the Site and Activity Center Levels," *Transit-Supportive Development in the United States: Experiences and Prospects*, Technology Sharing Program, U.S. Department of Transportation, Washington, D.C., 1993, pp. 60-126.

113 Some are *land planning/urban design manuals* with a transit orientation. Others are *transit facility design manuals* with implications for urban design. The former emphasize the needs of transit users accessing the system, the latter the needs of the transit operator running the system. R. Cervero, "Design Guidelines as a Tool to Promote Transit-Supportive Development," *Transit-Supportive Development in the United States: Experiences and Prospects*, Technology Sharing Program, U.S. Department of Transportation, Washington, D.C., 1993, pp. 27-40; and D. Everett, T. Herrero, and R. Ewing, *Transit-Oriented Development Guidelines: Review of Literature*, background paper prepared for the Florida Department of Transportation (FDOT), Tallahassee, 1995.

114 The local manuals are: Glatting Jackson Kercher Anglin Lopez Rinehart, Inc., *Central Florida Mobility Design Manual*, Central Florida Regional Transportation Authority, Orlando, 1994; Herbert - Halback, Inc., *Lynx: Customer Amenities Manual*, Central Florida Regional Transportation Authority, Orlando, 1994; and Lincks & Associates, Inc. et al., *Transit-Friendly Development*, Hillsborough Area Regional Transit Authority, Tampa, Fla., 1994. The statewide manual is: R. Ewing, *Pedestrian- and Transit-Friendly Design*, Florida Department of Transportation, Tallahassee, 1996b.

115 They are, respectively, E. Beimborn and H. Rabinowitz, *Guidelines for Transit-Sensitive Suburban Land Use Design*, Technology Sharing Program, U.S. Department of Transportation, Washington, D.C., 1991; and P. Calthorpe, *The Next American Metropolis: Ecology, Community, and the American Dream*, Princeton Architectural Press, New York, 1993, pp. 77-112. The latter represents the culmination of work begun by Calthorpe in Sacramento County, California, and later refined in San Diego, California, and Portland, Oregon.

116 The 7 unit-per-acre standard originated with an influential study of transit use in the New York region circa 1975. B.S. Pushkarev and J.M. Zupan, *Public Transportation and Land Use Policy*, Indiana University Press, Bloomington, 1977, pp. 137-148.

117 From ridership equations derived for Metro-Dade County (Miami), a residential density of 8.4 units per acre is required to achieve the operator's minimum transit productivity standard, that is, one-half the systemwide average passengers per revenue hour. From the same equations, a residential density of 14.3 units per acre is required to achieve the systemwide average productivity. Messinger and Ewing, op. cit.

118 For the status of transit-oriented development nationally, see M. Bernick and P. Hall, *New Emphasis on Transit-Based Housing Thoughout the United States*, National Transit Access Center, University of California at Berkeley, 1992; R.T. Dunphy, "Tranportation-Oriented Development: Making a Difference?" *Urban Land*, Vol. 54, July 1995, pp. 32-36 and 48; S. Jeer, "The Density Issue," *Planning*, Vol. 61, January 1995, p. 21; R.T. Dunphy, "New Developments in Light Rail," *Urban Land*, Vol. 55, July 1996, pp. 37-41 and 87; D. Salvesen, "Promoting Transit-Oriented Development," Vol. 55, July 1996, pp. 31-35 and 87; M. Bernick and R. Cervero, *Transit Villages in the 21st Century*, McGraw-Hill, New York, 1997; and D.R. Porter, *Transit-Focused Development*, Transit Cooperative Research Program Synthesis of Transit Practice 20, Transportation Research Board, Washington, D.C., 1997.

119 Reporting a relationship between land use mix and transit mode share are: Cambridge Systematics, op. cit., 1994a; Cervero, op. cit., 1996a; and Cervero and Kockelman, op. cit. Finding little or no relationship, once density is controlled, are: Frank and Pivo, op. cit.; Kitamura et al., op. cit.; and Ewing, op. cit., 1996b, pp. 83-93. As researchers are fond of saying, this is one of those subjects that begs for more funded research.

120 Beimborn and Rabinowitz, op. cit., Appendix A; Snohomish County Transportation Authority, *A Guide to Land Use and Public Transportation*, Technology Sharing Program, U.S. Department of Transportation, Washington, D.C., 1989, pp. 3-8 and 3-9; and Tri-County Metropolitan Transportation District of Oregon, *Planning and Design for Transit*, Portland, 1993, pp. 108-109.

121 For a compilation of transit-friendly land use regulations from around the U.S., see M. Morris, *Creating Transit-Supportive Land-Use Regulations: A Compendium of Codes, Standards, and Guidelines*, American Planning Association, Chicago, 1996. For the status of transit-oriented developments nationwide, see Bernick and Cervero, op. cit., 1994; Bernick and Cervero, op. cit., 1997; Dunphy, op. cit.; S. Jeer, "Zoning for Transit: A New Orientation," *Zoning News*, September 1994, pp. 1-4; R.T. Dunphy, "New Developments in Light Rail," *Urban Land*, Vol. 55, July 1996, pp. 37-41 and 87; D. Salvesen, "Promoting Transit-Oriented Development," Vol. 55, July 1996, pp. 31-35 and 87; and D.R. Porter, *Transit-Focused Development*, Transit Cooperative Research Program Synthesis of Transit Practice 20, Transportation Research Board, Washington, D.C., 1997.

122 The integration of bicycle and transit modes is the subject of M. Replogle, *Bicycles and Public Transportation: New Links to Suburban Transit Markets*, Bicycle Federation, Washington, D.C., 1983; and M. Replogle and H. Parcells, *Linking Bicycle/Pedestrian Facilities with Transit*, Case Study No. 9, National Bicycle and Walking Study, Federal Highway Administration, Washington, D.C., 1992.

123 D.A. Newman and M. Bebendorf, *Integrating Bicycles and Transit in Santa Barbara, California*, Office of Service and Methods Demonstration, U.S. Department of Transportation, Washington, D.C., 1983.

124 J. Al-Kazily, "Analysis of Park-and-Ride Lot Use in the Sacramento Region," *Transportation Research Record 1321*, 1991, pp. 1-6. Also see U.R. Abdus-Samad and W.L. Grecco, *Predicting Park'N Ride Parking Demand*, Joint Highway Research Project, Purdue University, West Lafayette, Ind., 1972; G.T. Baehr, "Park an Ride: Lots of Success," *Mass Transit*, Vol. 9, 1982, pp. 6-7, 48-49, and 54; M.N. Aronson and W.S. Homburger, *The Location and Design of Safe and Convenient Park-and-Ride Lots*, Institute of Transportation Studies, University of California at Berkeley, 1983; Federal Highway Administration (FHWA), *Park and Ride Facilities: Guidelines for Planning, Design and Operation*, Washington, D.C., 1986; G.S. Rutherford and C.A. Wellander, "Cost-Effectiveness of Park-and-Ride Lots in the Seattle Metropolitan Area," *Transportation Research Record 1081*, 1986, pp. 1-7; Frederic R. Harris, Inc., *State Park & Ride Lot Program: Planning Manual*, Florida Department of Transportation, Tallahassee, 1989; "The Best Park-and-Ride Lots, Part I," *The Urban Transportation Monitor*, April 13, 1990, pp. 10-11; D. Bolger, D. Colquhoun, and J. Morrall, "Planning and Design of Park-and-Ride Facilities for the Calgary Light Rail Transit System," *Transportation Research Record 1361*, 1992, pp. 141-148; and R.J. Spillar, R. Kinchen, and Y. Dehghani, "Models for Park-and-Ride Demand Estimation: A Seattle Experience," paper presented at the 75th Annual Meeting, Transportation Research Board, Washington, D.C., 1996.

125 W.E. Hurrell, A.A. Sgourakis, and S.B. Colman, "Application of Siting and Demand Estimation Model to Coordinate Park-and-Ride/HOV Facility Planning," *ITE 1994 Compendium of Technical Papers*, Institute of Transportation Engineers, Washington, D.C., 1994, pp. 354-358.

126 Abdus-Samad and Grecco, op. cit.; and Hurrell et al., op. cit. For design guidelines, see American Association of State Highway and Transportation Officials (AASHTO), *Guide for the Design of Park-and-Ride Facilities*, Washington, D.C., 1992; and K.F. Turnbull, *Effective Use of Park-and-Ride Facilities*, National Cooperative Highway Research Program Synthesis of Highway Practice 213, Transportation Research Board, Washington, D.C., 1995, pp. 21-26.

127 The statewide average utilization rate, 44 percent of available spaces, masks

tremendous variation across lots. Eleven lots have utilization rates over 80 percent, which is excellent. On the other hand, more lots have utilization rates under 10 percent.

128 S. Algers, S. Hansen, and G. Tegran, "Role of Waiting Time, Comfort and Convenience in Modal Choice for the Work Trip," *Transportation Research Record 534*, 1975, pp. 38-51; A.J. Horowitz, "Subjective Value of Time in Bus Transit Travel," *Transportation*, Vol. 10, 1981, 149-164; J.D. Hunt, "A Logit Model of Public Transport Route Choice," *ITE Journal*, Vol. 60, December 1990, pp. 26-30; and K. Quackenbush, J. McClennen, and J. Gallagher, "Transfer Penalties in Mode Choice Decisions," in J.M. Faris (ed.), *Proceedings of the Fifth Conference on Transportation Planning Methods—Volume II*, Transportation Research Board, Washington, D.C., 1995, pp. 23-17 through 23-27.

129 G.L. Thompson, "Planning Considerations for Alternative Transit Route Structures," *Journal of the American Institute of Planners*, Vol. 43, 1977, pp. 158-168; J.B. Schneider, *Transit and the Polycentric City*, Office of Technology Sharing, U.S. Department of Transportation, Washington, D.C., 1981; and E.J. Washington and R.W. Stokes, *Planning Guidelines for Suburban Transit Services*, Technology Sharing Program, U.S. Department of Transportation, Washington, D.C., 1988.

130 V.R. Vuchic, R. Clarke, and A.M. Molinero, *Timed Transfer System Planning, Design and Operation*, Urban Mass Transportation Administration, Washington, D.C., 1981, pp. 36-71.

131 Cervero, op. cit., 1994. Also see M. Kyte, K. Stanley, and E. Gleason, "Planning, Implementing, and Evaluating a Timed-Transfer System in Portland, Oregon," *Transportation Research Record 877*, 1982, pp. 23-29; J. Schneider, "The Timed-Transfer/Transit Center Concept as Applied in Tacoma/Pierce County, Washington," *Transportation Quarterly*, Vol. 38, July 1984, pp. 393-402; J. Bakker et al., "Multi-Centered Time Transfer System for Capital Metro, Austin, Texas," *Transportation Research Record 1202*, 1988, pp. 22-28; and J.B. Schneider et al., *Planning, Designing and Operating Multi-Center Timed-Transfer Transit Systems: Guidelines from Recent Experience with Six Cities*, Urban Mass Transportation Administration, Washington, D.C., 1994.

132 Systan, Inc., *Timed Transfer: An Evaluation of Its Structure, Performance and Cost*, Urban Mass Transportation Administration, Washington, D.C., 1983, pp. xxi-xxii.

133 T.M. Batz, *High Occupancy Vehicle Treatments, Impacts and Parameters - Volume II*, Federal Highway Administration (FHWA), Washington, D.C., 1986; JHK & Associates, "HOV Treatments in Downtown Areas," in *Strategies to Alleviate Traffic Congestion*, Institute of Transportation Engineers, Washington, D.C., 1987, pp. 505-514; H.S. Levinson, "HOV Lanes on Arterial Streets," in *Proceedings of the Second National Conference on High-Occupancy Vehicle Lanes and Transitways*, Office of Technology Sharing, U.S. Department of Transportation, Washington, D.C., 1987, pp. 105-125; "Arterial Street HOV Applications," in K.F. Turnbull (ed.), *Sixth National Conference on High-Occupancy Vehicle Systems*, Transportation Research Board, Washington, D.C., 1993, pp. 41-43; K.L. Jacobson, L. Ingalls, and E.H. Melone, "Alternatives for Providing Priority to High-Occupancy Vehicles in the Suburban Operating Environment," *Transportation Research Record 1394*, 1993, pp. 59-64; B. Huddy (presider), "Arterial HOV Treatments," *Seventh National Conference on High-Occupancy Vehicle Systems*, Transportation Research Board, Washington, D.C., 1994, pp. 81-84; and V. Vuchic and S. Kikuchi, *The Bus Transit System: Its Underutilized Potential*, Technology Sharing Program, U.S. Department of Transportation, Washington, D.C., 1994, pp. 11-16.

134 J.A. Cracknell and D. Case, "Bus Priority Techniques," in *Public Transport Planning and Operations*, PTRC Education and Research Services Ltd., London, 1992, pp. 141-152. Also see D.C. Royer, "Integrating Transit and Urban Street Operations in the City of Los Angeles," *ITE 1990 Compendium of Technical Papers*, Institute of Transportation Engineers, Washington, D.C., 1990, pp. 12-13; W.C. Kloos, A.R. Danaher, and K.M. Hunter-Zaworski, "Bus Priority at Traffic Signals in Portland: The Powell Boulevard Pilot Project," *ITE 1994 Compendium of Technical Papers*, Institute of Transportation Engineers, Washington, D.C., 1994, pp. 420-424; A.S. Shalaby and R.M. Soberman, "Effect of With-Flow Bus Lanes on Bus Travel Times," *Transportation Research Record 1433*, 1994, pp. 24-30; G. Robbins and J. Mirabdal, "Improving Transit Speeds Through Traffic Engineering Measures," *ITE 1995 Compendium of Technical Papers*, Institute of Transportation Engineers, Washington, D.C., 1995, pp. 494-497; B.F. Boje and M. Nookala, "Signal Priority for Buses: An Operational Test at Louisiana Avenue, Minneapolis," *ITE 1996 Compendium of Technical Papers*, Institute of Transportation Engineers, Washington, D.C., 1996, pp. 309-313; A.M. Stoddard, "Development of Arterial High-Occupancy-Vehicle Lane Enforcement Techniques," *Transportation Research Record 1554*, 1996, pp. 128-135; and D. Watry and J. Mirabdal, "Transit Preferential Streets Program in San Francisco," *ITE 1996 Compendium of Technical Papers*, Institute of Transportation Engineers, Washington, D.C., 1996, pp. 314-318.

135 JHK & Associates, op. cit., 1987; Levinson, op. cit; V. Patterson, "Preferential Treatment of Buses: Reserved Lanes on Urban Streets," *ITE 1988 Compendium of Technical Papers*, Institute of Transportation Engineers, Washington, D.C., 1988, pp.

290-294; N.L. Nihan, J.E. Davis, and L.N. Jacobson, "High-Occupancy Vehicle Improvements on Signalized Arterials," *ITE Journal*, Vol. 61, March 1991, pp. 15-19; American Association of State Highway and Transportation Officials (AASHTO), *Guide for the Design of High Occupancy Vehicle Facilities*, Washington, D.C., 1991, pp. 23-58 (freeways) and 59-81 (surface streets); and S.M. Turner, "High-Occupancy Vehicle Treatments on Arterial Streets," *ITE Journal*, Vol. 63, November 1993, pp. 22-29.

136 H.S. Rose and D.H. Hinds, "South Dixie Highway Contraflow Bus and Car-Pool Lane Demonstration Project," *Transportation Research Record 606*, 1976, pp. 18-22; and M.J. Rothenberg, *Priority Treatment for High Occupancy Vehicles: Project Status Report*, Federal Highway Administration, Washington, D.C., 1977, pp. 22-23.

137 B.C. Fowler, "The South Dade Busway," *ITE 1995 Compendium of Technical Papers*, Institute of Transportation Engineers, Washington, D.C., 1995, pp. 508-511.

138 Batz, op. cit.; Vuchic and Kikuchi, op. cit.; ITE Technical Council Committee 6A-37, *The Effectiveness of High-Occupancy Vehicle Facilities*, Institute of Transportation Engineers, Washington, D.C., 1988; L. Newman, C. Nuworsoo, and A.D. May, "Operational and Safety Experience with Freeway Facilities in California," *Transportation Research Record 1173*, 1988, pp. 18-24; K.F. Turnbull and J.W. Hanks, *A Description of High-Occupancy Vehicle Facilities in North America*, Technology Sharing Program, U.S. Department of Transportation, Washington, D.C., 1990; K.F. Turnbull, *An Assessment of High Occupancy Vehicle (HOV) Facilities in North America: Executive Report*, Technology Sharing Program, U.S. Department of Transportation, Washington, D.C., 1991; K.F. Turnbull, *High-Occupancy Vehicle Project Case Studies: Historical Trends and Project Experiences*, Technology Sharing Program, U.S. Department of Transportation, Washington, D.C., 1991; J.F. Kain, *Increasing the Productivity of the Nation's Urban Transportation Infrastructure: Measures to Increase Transit Use and Carpooling*, Technology Sharing Program, U.S. Department of Transportation, Washington, D.C., 1992, pp. 15-1 through 15-15; C.A. Fuhs, *Preferential Lane Treatments for High-Occupancy Vehicles*, National Cooperative Highway Research Program Synthesis 185, Transportation Research Board, Washington, D.C., 1993; K.F. Turnbull, *More for Less with HOV: The Benefits of High-Occupancy Vehicle Projects*, Institute of Transportation Engineers, Washington, D.C., 1993; and J.W. Emerson and S.G. Strickland, "HOV Facilities: Status and National Perspective," *ITE 1994 Compendium of Technical Papers*, Institute of Transportation Engineers, Washington, D.C., 1994, pp. 70-73.

139 C. Fuhs, "Enforcement Issues Associated with HOV Facilities," in K.F. Turnbull (ed.), *Fifth National High-Occupancy Vehicle (HOV) Facilities Conference*, Transportation Research Board, Washington, D.C., 1991, pp. 251-290. Also see C. Ulberg and E.L. Jacobson, *HOV Lane Enforcement Evaluation*, Washington State Transportation Center, University of Washington, Seattle, 1993; "HOV-Lane Enforcement Schemes Evaluated," *Texas Transportation Researcher*, Vol. 30, Spring 1994, pp. 10-11; and J.W. Billheimer (presider), "Enforcement Issues," *Seventh National Conference on High-Occupancy Vehicle Systems*, Transportation Research Board, Washington, D.C., 1994, pp. 64-67

140 Mode shifts begin to occur when travel time savings exceed five minutes. A. Mogharabi, "Forecasting the Demand for HOV Lanes," *ITE 1991 Compendium of Technical Papers*, Institute of Transportation Engineers, Washington, D.C., 1991, pp. 561-566. Other recent studies of commuter response to HOV lanes include B.S. McMullen and T. Gut, "HOV Lane Effectiveness in Controlling Traffic Congestion," *Transportation Quarterly*, Vol. 46, 1992, 429-434; G. Farnsworth and G.C. Ulberg, "Evaluation of Seattle's South I-5 Interim High-Occupancy Vehicle Lanes," *Transportation Research Record 1394*, 1993, pp. 65-72; M.J. Poppe, D.J.P. Hook, and K.M. Howell, "Evaluation of High-Occupancy-Vehicle Lanes in Phoenix, Arizona," *Transportation Research Record 1446*, 1994, pp. 1-7; G.E. Gray et al., "Caltrans Interstate 15 Reversible High-Occupancy Lanes: 1994 Status," *Transportation Research Record 1494*, 1995, pp. 48-58; and A. Pint et al., "Evaluation of the Minnesota I-394 HOV Transportation System," *Transportation Research Record 1494*, 1995, pp. 59-66.

141 R.H. Henk, D.L. Christiansen, and T.J. Lomax, "Simplified Approach for Estimating the Cost-Effectiveness of HOV Facilities," *Transportation Research Record 1299*, 1991, pp. 28-39.

142 J. Gard, P.P. Jovanis, and R. Kitamura, "Factors Influencing Public Support for Converting a Mixed-Use Freeway Lane into an HOV Lane," paper presented at the 74th Annual Meeting, Transportation Research Board, Washington, D.C., 1995.

143 For an overview of the project, see Pint et al., op. cit.; and G.A. Finstad, "Garages: The Key to a Successful Transportation System," *ITE Journal*, Vol. 66, May 1996, pp. 38-42.

144 J.L. Wright and F.O. Robinson, "Travlink: Can Information Influence Choice," *Proceedings of the 1993 Annual Meeting of IVHS America*, IVHS America, Washington, D.C., 1993, pp. 89-93.

145 Niagara Frontier Transportation Authority, "Privatization Experience of Other

Cities' Transit Systems," *Transit Contracting Services Study*, Buffalo, N.Y., pp. D-1 through D-27; and S. Rosenbloom, *Developing a Comprehensive Strategy to Meet a Range of Suburban Travel Needs*, Urban Mass Transportation Administration, U.S. Department of Transportation, Washington, D.C., 1990, pp. 18-30 and 57-95.

146 American Public Transit Association (APTA), *Transit Fare Summary*, Washington, D.C., 1995, pp. 470-472.

147 P.R. White and R.P. Turner, "Development of Intensive Urban Minibus Services in Britain," *Logistics and Transportation Review*, Vol. 23, 1987, pp. 385-400; J.J. McLary, A. Stahl, and S. Persich, "Implementation of Service Routes in the United States," *Transportation Research Record 1378*, 1993, pp. 21-27; and EG&G Dynatrend and Crain & Associates, *Evaluating Transit Operations for Individuals with Disabilities*, Transit Cooperative Research Program, Transportation Research Board, Washington, D.C., January 1995 draft, pp. II-1 through II-40 and IV-1 through IV-15.

148 White and Turner, op. cit.; and S.J. Andrle, F. Spielberg, and A. Hungerbuhler, *Operating Costs and Characteristics of Minibuses*, Urban Mass Transportation Administration, U.S. Department of Transportation, Washington, D.C., 1981, pp. 17-47.

149 Most cities have opted for service routes that wind through neighborhoods and stop at apartment complexes, shopping centers, health clinics, and bus transfer points. Two cities, Sunrise and Cooper City, have gone even further toward total demand responsiveness with "point deviation" and "route deviation" services, respectively. For descriptions and performance data, see Project ACTION, *Broward County, Florida—Transit Options Project: Development of Local Community Bus Services*, Washington, D.C., 1995, pp. 13-32.

150 J. Pucher and I. Hirschman, *Path to Balanced Transportation: Expand Public Transportation Services and Require Auto Users to Pay the Full Social, Environmental and Economic Costs of Driving*, Rutgers University, New Brunswick, N.J., 1993, pp. 15-18.

151 G.E. Peterson, W.G. Davis, and C. Walker, *Total Compensation of Mass Transit Employees in Large Metropolitan Areas*, The Urban Institute, Washington, D.C., 1986, pp. 13-27; and American Public Transit Association (APTA), *1994-1995 Transit Fact Book*, Washington, D.C., 1995, p. 57.

152 S.R. Mundle, J.E. Kraus, and G.A. Hoge, "Impact of Labor Contract Provisions on Transit Operator Productivity," *Transportation Research Record 1266*, 1990, pp. 23-30.

153 From the FY 1994 National Transit Database, peak periods (typically 6:00-9:00 a.m. and 3:30-6:30 p.m.) represent between 40 and 75 percent of average weekday bus ridership, depending on the city.

154 Costly work rules include maximum spread times on split shifts, spread premiums on top of base pay, limitations on the number of split shifts, and guaranteed full pay for less than a full day's work.

155 K.M. Chomitz and C.A. Lave, *Part-Time Labor, Work Rules, and Transit Costs*, Urban Mass Transportation Administration, U.S. Department of Transportation, Washington, D.C., 1981, pp. 49-60; and K.M. Chomitz and C.A. Lave, "Forecasting the Financial Effects of Work Rule Changes," *Transportation Quarterly*, Vol. 37, 1983, pp. 453-473. Also see A.K. Bladikas and C. Papadimitriou, "Analysis of Bus Transit's Operating Labor Efficiency Using Section 15 Data," *Transportation Research Record 1013*, 1985, pp. 49-57.

156 K. Chomitz, G. Giuliano, and C. Lave, "Part-Time Public Transit Operators: Experiences and Prospects," *Transportation Research Record 1013*, 1985, pp. 32-38; C.A. Lave, "Absenteeism, Accidents, and Attrition: Part-Time Versus Full-Time Bus Drivers," *Transportation Research Record 1078*, 1986, pp. 62-71; and L.C. MacDorman, *Use of Part-Time Operators*, Synthesis of Transit Practice 9, National Cooperative Transit Research & Development Program, Transportation Research Board, Washington, D.C., 1986, pp. 17-20.

157 For arguments pro and con, see R. Cervero, *Transit Service Contracting: Cream-Skimming or Deficit-Skimming?*, Technology Sharing Program, U.S. Department of Transportation, 1988; E.D. Sclar, K.H. Schaeffer, and R. Brandwein, *The Emperor's New Clothes: Transit Privatization and Public Policy*, Economic Policy Institute, Washington, D.C., 1989; W. Cox and J. Love, *A Public Purpose for Public Transit*, Reason Foundation, Los Angeles, 1990; A. Black, "Privatization of Urban Transit: A Different Perspective," *Transportation Research Record 1297*, 1991, pp. 69-75; E.D. Sclar, *Less Than Meets the Eye: Colorado's Costly Experience with Transit Privatization*, Economic Policy Institute, Washington, D.C., 1991; R.L. Peskin, S.R. Mundle, and S.D. Buhrer, "Transit Privatization in Denver: Experience in First Year," *Transportation Research Record 1349*, 1992, pp. 75-84; J.A. Gomez-Ibanez and J.R. Meyer, *Going Private: The International Experience with Transport Privatization*, The Brookings Institution, Washington, D.C., 1993, pp. 62-83; J. Love and W. Cox, *Competitive*

Contracting of Transit Services, Reason Foundation, Los Angeles, 1993; and R.L. Peskin, S.R. Mundle, and P.K. Varma, "Transit Privatization in Denver: Experience in the Second Year," *Transportation Research Record 1402*, 1993, pp. 17-24.

158 R.F. Teal, "Issues Raised by Competitive Contracting of Bus Transit Service in the USA," *Transportation Planning and Technology*, Vol. 15, 1991, pp. 391-403.

159 Teal, op. cit. Also see Carter-Goble Associates, Inc., *Cost Reduction and Service Improvements from Contracting in Rural, Small Urban, and Suburban Areas*, Technology Sharing Program, U.S. Department of Transportation, Washington, D.C., 1987, pp. i-iii; and Center for Urban Transportation Research (CUTR), *Privatization in Mass Transit: Technical Memorandum #2*, University of South Florida, Tampa, 1993a, pp. 3-25.

160 Love and Cox, op. cit., pp. 7-16; ATE Management and Service Company, Inc., *Private Sector Contracting for Transit Services: Operator Handbook*, Urban Mass Transportation Adminstration, U.S. Department of Transportation, 1987; W. Cox and J. Love, *Designing Public Transit Competitive Contracting Programs: The Public Perspective*, American Bus Association, Washington, D.C., 1988; DeLoitte & Touche, *Guidelines for Public Transportation Contracting with the Private Sector in California: Manual*, California Department of Transportation, Sacramento, 1990; and Center of Urban Transportation Research (CUTR), *Transit Service Contracting: A Handbook for Florida's Transit Systems*, Florida Department of Transportation, Tallahassee, 1993b.

161 Gomez-Ibanez and Meyer, op. cit., pp. 73-74.

162 W.R. Talley, "Contracting Out and Cost Economies for a Public Transit Firm," *Transportation Quarterly*, Vol. 45, 1991, pp. 409-420; and ITE Technical Council Committee 6A-41, *Privatization of Public Transit Services*, Institute of Transportation Engineers, Washington, D.C., 1992, pp. 13-21.

163 Carter-Goble Associates, Inc., op. cit.

164 Center for Urban Transportation Research (CUTR), op. cit., 1993a, p. 6.

165 Untermann, op. cit., p. 1.

166 All but five of the 100 cities and towns fall in the size range of 10,000 to 100,000 population.

167 Greenways Incorporated, *Current Planning Guidelines and Design Standards Being Used By State and Local Agencies for Bicycle and Pedestrian Facilities*, Case Study No. 24, National Bicycling and Walking Study, Federal Highway Administration, Washington, D.C., 1992, p. 8. This conclusion is reiterated in ITE Technical Committee 6A-55, *Review of Planning Guidelines and Design Standards for Bicycle Facilities*, Institute of Transportation Engineers, Washington, D.C., 1997, p. 5.

168 S.A. Smith et al., *Planning and Implementing Pedestrian Facilities in Suburban and Developing Rural Areas*, National Cooperative Highway Research Program Report 294A, Transportation Research Board, Washington, D.C., 1987, pp. 27-28.

169 From a special tabulation of the 1990 Nationwide Personal Transportation Survey (NPTS), 72 percent of the work trips by bicycle are two miles or less; the comparable figure for shopping trips is 87 percent.

170 F.O. Robinson, J.L. Edwards, and C.E. Ohrn, "Strategies for Increasing Levels of Walking and Bicycling for Utilitarian Purposes," *Transportation Research Record 743*, 1980, pp. 38-48. Also see Cervero, 1996a; Cervero and Kockelman, op. cit., 1996; Handy, op. cit., 1992; Handy, op. cit., 1993; Handy, op. cit., 1995; and Handy, op. cit., 1996.

171 A. Polus and A. Katz, "An Analysis of Nighttime Pedestrian Accidents at Specially Illuminated Crosswalks," *Accident Analysis and Prevention*, Vol. 10, 1978, pp. 223-228; R.N. Schwab et al., "Roadway Lighting," in *Synthesis of Safety Research Related to Traffic Control and Roadway Elements—Volume 2*, Federal Highway Administration, Washington, D.C., 1982, pp. 12-2 through 12-6; C.V. Zegeer, K.S. Opiela, and M.J. Cynecki, "Effect of Pedestrian Signals and Signal Timing on Pedestrian Accidents, *Transportation Research Record 847*, 1982, pp. 62-72; H.N. Tobey, E.M. Shunamen, and R.L. Knoblauch, *Pedestrian Trip Making Characteristics and Exposure Measures*, Federal Highway Administration, Washington, D.C., 1983, pp. 74-75; C.V. Zegeer, K.S. Opiela, and M.J. Cynecki, *Pedestrian Signalization Alternatives: Final Report*, Turner-Fairbank Highway Research Center, McLean, Va., 1985, pp. 33-43; R.L. Knoblauch et al., *Investigation of Exposure Based Pedestrian Accident Areas: Crosswalks, Sidewalks, Local Streets and Major Arterials*, Federal Highway Administration, Washington, D.C., 1988, pp. 126-133; N.J. Garber and R. Srinivasan, *Accident Characteristics of Elderly Pedestrians*, Mid-Atlantic Universities Transportation Center, University Park, Pa., 1990; C.V. Zegeer, *Synthesis of Safety Research: Pedestrians*, Federal Highway Administration, Washington, D.C., 1991, pp. 38-50; C.V. Zegeer, J.C. Stutts, and W.W. Hunter, *Safety Effectiveness of Highway Design Features—Volume VI: Pedestrians and Bicyclists*, Federal Highway Administration,

Washington, D.C., 1992, pp. 10-13; B.L. Bowman and R.L. Vecellio, *Investigation of the Impact of Medians on Road Users*, Federal Highway Administration, Washington, D.C., 1994, pp. 36-54; B.L. Bowman and R.L. Vecellio, "An Assessment of Current Practice in the Selection and Design of Urban Medians to Benefit Pedestrians," *Transportation Research Record 1445*, 1994, pp. 180-189; and B.L. Bowman and R.L. Vecellio, "Effect of Urban and Suburban Median Types on Both Vehicular and Pedestrian Safety," *Transportation Research Record 1445*, 1994, pp. 169-179.

172 Forester, op. cit., pp. 127-144; C.L. Antonakos, "Environmental and Travel Preferences of Cyclists," *Transportation Research Record 1438*, 1994, pp. 25-33; W.W. Hunter and H.F. Huang, "User Counts on Bicycle Lanes and Multi-Use Trails in the United States," *Transportation Research Record 1504*, 1995, pp. 45-57; and D. Taylor and H. Mahmassani, "Analysis of Stated Preferences for Intermodal Bicycle-Transit Interfaces," *Transportation Research Record 1556*, 1996, pp. 86-95.

173 A comparison of cities with high and low levels of bicycle commuting found that the former have six times as many *bike lane miles per arterial road mile* as the latter. S.A. Goldsmith, *Reasons Why Bicycling and Walking Are and Are Not Being Used More Extensively as Travel Modes*, Federal Highway Administration, Washington, D.C., 1992, pp. 39-42 and 54-56. Also see D.T. Smith, *Safety and Locational Criteria for Bicycle Facilities: Final Report*, Federal Highway Administration, Washington, D.C., 1975, pp. 24-29 and 56-72; D.F. Lott and D.Y. Lott, "Effect of Bike Lanes on Ten Classes of Bicycle-Automobile Accidents in Davis, California," *Journal of Safety Research*, Vol. 8, 1976, pp. 171-179; B. Kroll and M.R. Ramey, "Effects of Bike Lanes on Driver and Bicyclist Behavior," *Transportation Engineering Journal*, Vol. , 1977, pp. 243-256; City of Eugene, *Bicycles in Cities: The Eugene Experience*, Eugene, Ore., 1981; B. Kroll and R. Sommer, "Bicyclists' Response to Urban Bikeways," in H.S. Levinson and R.A. Weant (eds.), *Urban Transportation: Perspectives and Prospects*, Eno Transportation Foundation, Landsdowne, Va., 1982, pp. 245-252; S.R. McHenry and M.J. Wallace, *Evaluation of Wide Curb Lanes as Shared Lane Bicycle Facilities*, Maryland Department of Transportation, Baltimore, 1985,, pp. 39-63; S.I. Badgett, D.A. Niemeier, and G.S. Rutherford, "Bicycle Commuting Deterrents and Incentives: A Survey of Selected Companies in the Greater Seattle Area," paper presented at the 73rd Annual Meeting, Transportation Research Board, Washington, D.C., 1994; and A. Sorton and T. Walsh, "Urban and Suburban Compatibility Street Evaluation Using Bicycle Stress Level," paper presented at the 73rd Annual Meeting, Transportation Research Board, Washington, D.C., 1994.

174 The Bicycle Federation of America estimates that fewer than 5 percent of all bicyclists qualify as experienced or highly skilled. W.C. Wilkinson et al., op. cit., p. 1.

175 M.D. Everett and J. Spencer, "Empirical Evidence on Determinants of Mass Bicycle Commuting in the United States: A Cross-Community Analysis," *Transportation Research Record 912*, 1983, pp. 28-37.

176 Greenways Incorporated, op. cit., pp. 20-57; and ITE Technical Committee 6A-55, op. cit., pp. 10-37.

177 American Association of State Highway and Transportation Officials (AASHTO), *Guide for Development of Bicycle Facilities*, Washington, D.C., 1991.

178 Seminal works on pedestrian-friendly design include: Lynch and Hack, op. cit., pp. 153-222; Untermann, op. cit., 1984, pp. 173-229; J. Jacobs, *The Death and Life of Great American Cities*, Random House, New York, 1961; C. Alexander, S. Ishikawa, and M. Silverstein, *A Pattern Language: Towns-Buildings-Construction*, Oxford University Press, New York, 1977 (particularly Patterns 22-25, 30-32, 51-55, 60-61, 97-103, 106, and 119-123); various articles in S. Anderson (ed.), *On Streets*, MIT Press, Cambridge, Mass., 1986; W.H. Whyte, *City: Rediscovering the Center*, Doubleday, New York, 1988, pp. 68-140; A. Rapoport, *History and Precedent in Environmental Design*, Plenum Press, New York, 1990, pp. 243-282, 453-467; various articles in A.V. Moudon (ed.), *Public Streets for Public Use*, Columbia University Press, New York, 1991; and A.B. Jacobs, *Great Streets*, MIT Press, Cambridge, Mass., 1993, pp. 271-314.

179 D. Zevin, "America's 10 Best," *Walking*, August 1991, pp. 41- 52. The 10 best are: San Francisco; Savannah, Ga.; Washington, D.C.; Portland, Ore.; Boulder, Colo.; New York; Boston; Chicago; Philadelphia; and New Orleans.

180 S. Martin, "The 10 Best Cities for Cycling (Plus a Few Others You Should Only Drive Through)," *Bicycling*, April 1990, pp. 61-68, 73. The 10 best are, in order, Seattle; Palo Alto, Calif.; San Diego; Boulder, Colo.; Davis, Calif.; Gainesville, Fla.; Eugene, Ore.; Montreal; Madison, Wis.; and Missoula, Mont.

181 C. Buchanan, "Appendix A: The Environmental Capacity of Streets," *Traffic in Towns: A Study of the Long Term Problems of Traffic in Urban Areas*, Her Majesty's Stationery Office, London, 1963, pp. 203-213; H. Marks, "Traffic Capacity," *Traffic Circulation Planning for Communities*, Gruen Associates, Los Angeles, 1974, pp. 223-231; D. Appleyard, *Livable Streets*, University of California Press, Berkeley, 1981, pp. 41-99; D.T. Smith and D. Appleyard, "Studies of Speed and Volume on Residential Streets," *Improving the Residential Street Environment*, Federal Highway Administration, Washington, D.C., 1981, pp. 113-130; S. Spitz, "How Much Traffic Is Too Much

(Traffic)," *ITE Journal*, Vol. 52, May 1982, pp. 44-45; TEST, *Quality Streets: How Traditional Urban Centres Benefit from Traffic-Calming*, London, 1988, pp. 1-20; R. Klaeboe, "Measuring the Environmental Impact of Road Traffic in Town Areas," in *Environmental Issues*, PTRC Education and Research Services Ltd., London, England, 1992, pp. 81-88; and L.N. Dallam, "Environmental Capacity of Neighborhood Streets," *ITE 1996 Compendium of Technical Papers*, Institute of Transportation Engineers, Washington, D.C., 1996, pp. 422-423.

182 The foreign experience is reviewed in a special issue of *Built Environment* (Vol. 12, No. 1/2, 1986); R. Tolley, *Calming Traffic in Residential Areas*, Brefi Press, Brefi, England, 1990; County Surveyors Society, *Traffic Calming in Practice*, Landor Publishing, London, 1994; and R. Brindle, *Living with Traffic*, ARRB Transport Research Ltd., Victoria, Australia, 1995. Other reports on traffic calming outside North America include R. Sumner and C. Baguley, *Speed Control Humps on Residential Roads*, Transport and Road Research Lab, Crowthorne, England, 1979, pp. 3-10; M.R. Daff and I.D.K. Siggins, "On Road Trials of Some New Types of Slow Points," Vol. 11, 1982, pp. 214-237; M. Jenks, "Residential Roads Researched: Are Innovative Estates Safer?" *Architects' Journal*, Vol. 177, June 1983, pp. 46-49; M. Fager, "Environmental Traffic Management in Stockholm," *ITE Journal*, Vol. 54, July 1984, pp. 16-19; J.H. Kraay, M.P.M. Mathijssen, and F.C.M. Wegman, *Toward Safer Residential Areas*, Institute of Road Safety Research SWOV/Ministry of Transport, Leidschendam, Switzerland, 1985, pp. 30-39; H.H. Keller, "Urban and Transport Planning Concepts to Revitalise Two Medium-Sized Town Centres in West Germany," in *New Life for City Centres: Planning, Transport, and Conservation in British and German Cities*, Anglo-German Foundation for the Study of Industrial Society, London, 1988, pp. 179-185; TEST, *Quality Streets: How Traditional Urban Centres Benefit from Traffic-Calming*, London, 1988; CART, *Traffic Calming*, Sensible Transportation Options for People, Tigard, Ore., 1989; W.S. Homburger et al., *Residential Street Design and Traffic Control*, Prentice Hall, Englewood Cliffs, N.J., 1989, pp. 79-112; H.H. Keller, "Three Generations of Traffic Calming in the Federal Republic of Germany," *Environmental Issues*, PTRC Education and Research Services, Sussex, England, 1989, pp. 15-31; Devon County Council, *Traffic Calming Guidelines*, Great Britain, 1991; B. Eubanks-Ahrens, "A Closer Look at the Users of Woonerven," in A. Vernez Moudon (ed.), *Public Streets for Public Use*, Columbia University Press, New York, 1991, pp. 63-79; S.T. Janssen, "Road Safety in Urban Districts: Final Results of Accident Studies in the Dutch Demonstration Projects of the 1970s," *Traffic Engineering + Control*, Vol. 32, 1991, pp. 292-296; J. Marstrand et al., *Urban Traffic Areas - Part 7: Speed Reducers*, Vejdirektoratet - Vejregeludvalget, The Netherlands, 1991; S. Proctor, "Accident Reduction Through Area-Wide Traffic Schemes," *Traffic Engineering + Control*, No. 12, 1991, pp. 566-573; R. Brindle, "Local Street Speed Management in Australia: Is It 'Traffic Calming'?" *Accident Analysis and Prevention*, Vol. 24, 1992, pp. 29-38; S.D. Challis, "North Earlham Estate, Worwich: The First UK 20 mph Zone," in *Traffic Management and Road Safety*, PTRC Education and Research Services Ltd., London, England, 1992, pp. 61-72; M. Durkin and T. Pheby, "York: Aiming To Be the UK's First Traffic Calmed City," in *Traffic Management and Road Safety*, PTRC Education and Research Services Ltd., London, England, 1992, pp. 73-90; L. Herrstedt, "Traffic Calming Design: A Speed Management Method - Danish Experience on Environmentally Adapted Through Roads," *Accident Analysis and Prevention*, Vol. 24, 1992, pp. 3-16; J. Pucher and S. Clorer, "Taming the Automobile in Germany," *Transportation Quarterly*, Vol. 46, 1992, pp. 383-395; D. Zaidel, A.S. Hakkert, and A.H. Pistiner, "The Use of Road Humps for Moderating Speeds on Urban Streets," *Accident Analysis and Prevention*, Vol. 24, 1992, pp. 45-56; L. Herrstedt et al., *An Improved Traffic Environment? A Catalogue of Ideas*, Danish Road Directorate, Copenhagen, Denmark, 1993; W. Brilon and H. Blanke, "Extensive Traffic Calming: Results of the Accident Analyses in Six Model Towns," *ITE 1993 Compendium of Technical Papers*, Institute of Transportation Engineers, Washington, D.C., 1993, pp. 119-123; A. O'Brien, "Traffic Calming: Ideas Into Practice," *ITE 1993 Compendium of Technical Papers*, Institute of Transportation Engineers, Washington, D.C., 1993, pp. 129-134; and C.V. Zegeer et al., *FHWA Study Tour for Pedestrian and Bicyclist Safety in England, Germany, and The Netherlands*, Federal Highway Administration, Washington, D.C., 1994, pp. 38-41, 55-57, 69-73, and 81.

183 J. Craus et al., "Geometric Aspects of Traffic Calming in Shared Streets," *ITE 1993 Compendium of Technical Papers*, Institute of Transportation Engineers, Washington, D.C., 1993, pp. 1-5; K.L. Gonzalez, "Neighborhood Traffic Control: Bellevue's Approach," *ITE Journal*, Vol. 63, 1993, pp. 43-45; S. Grava, "Traffic Calming: Can It Be Done in America?" *Transportation Quarterly*, Vol. 47, 1993, pp. 483-505; M. Klik and A. Faghri, "A Comparative Evaluation of Speed Humps and Deviations," *Transportation Quarterly*, Vol. 47, 1993, pp. 457-469; A. Clarke and M.J. Dornfeld, *Traffic Calming, Auto-Restricted Zones and Other Traffic Management Techniques: Their Effects on Bicycling and Pedestrians*, Case Study No. 19, National Bicycling and Walking Study, Federal Highway Administration, Washington, D.C., 1994; R. Drdul and M. Skene, "Traffic Calming Do's and Don'ts," *ITE 1994 Compendium of Technical Papers*, Institute of Transportation Engineers, Washington, D.C., 1994, pp. 491-495; G. Halbert et al., "Implementation of a Residential Traffic Control Program in the City of San Diego," *Environment: Changing Our Transportation Priorities*, Institute of Transportation Engineers, Washington, D.C., 1994, pp. 265-271; K. Halperin and R. Huston, "A Verkehrsberuhigung Design for an American Road," *ITE Journal*, Vol. 64, April 1994, pp. 28-34; B.K. Kemper and P.M. Fernandez, "Neighborhood Traffic Control Measures," in *Design and Safety of Pedestrian Facilities*, Institute of Transpor-

tation Engineers, Washington, D.C., 1994, pp. 48-53; J.P. Savage, R.D. MacDonald, and J. Ewell, *A Guidebook for Residential Traffic Management*, Washington State Department of Transportation, Olympia, Wash., 1994; E. Ben-Joseph, "Changing the Residential Street Scene: Adapting the Shared Street (Woonerf) Concept to the Suburban Environment," *Journal of the American Planning Association*, Vol. 61, 1995, pp. 504-515; R.M. Burchfield, "Traffic Calming Collector Streets: Portland's Experience," *ITE 1995 Compendium of Technical Papers*, Institute of Transportation Engineers, Washington, D.C., 1995, pp. 67-69; various articles in *Traffic Calming*, Ontario Traffic Conference, Toronto, 1995; C.L. Hoyle, *Traffic Calming*, Planning Advisory Service Report Number 456, 1995, pp. 25-39; C.E. Walter, "Suburban Residential Traffic Calming," *ITE Journal*, Vol. 65, 1995, pp. 44-48; M. DeRobertis and A. Wachtel, "Traffic Calming: Do's and Don'ts to Encourage Bicycling," *ITE 1996 Compendium of Technical Papers*, Institute of Transportation Engineers, Washington, D.C., 1996, pp. 498-503; C. Hoyle and R. Ewing, "Traffic Calming for New Residential Streets Enhances Housing Value," *Land Development*, Vol. 9, Fall 1996, pp. 7-11; K. Ochia, "Calming Urban Street Crime through Traffic Calming: Program Development and Implementation," *ITE 1996 Compendium of Technical Papers*, Institute of Transportation Engineers, Washington, D.C., 1996, pp. 424-428; J.P. Perone, "Developing and Implementing Traffic Calming Warrants," *ITE 1996 Compendium of Technical Papers*, Institute of Transportation Engineers, Washington, D.C., 1996, pp. 351-353; and G.L. Ullman, "Neighborhood Speed Control: U.S. Practices," *ITE 1996 Compendium of Technical Papers*, Institute of Transportation Engineers, Washington, D.C., 1996, pp. 111-115. The international conference, to be held in Tampa in March 1997, will have one-third of the sessions devoted to traffic calming. A compendium, *Transportation and Sustainable Communities: Resource Papers*, will be available from ITE after the conference.

184 Ewing, op. cit., 1996a, pp. 62-65.

185 Hall Planning & Engineering (with R. Ewing), *Belleair Traffic Calming Plan: Final Report*, Belleair, Fla., 1996.

186 Florida Department of Transportation (FDOT), *Manual of Uniform Minimum Standards for Design, Construction, and Maintenance for Streets and Highways (The Green Book)*, Tallahassee.

187 RK & K Consulting Engineers (with R. Ewing), *Mobility Friendly Design Standards Study: Policy Guidelines for Local & Collector Streets*, prepared for Wilmington Area Planning Council and Delaware Department of Transportation, Wilmington, Del., 1997 draft.

188 The material in this chapter has been published before in R. Ewing, "Measuring Transportation Performance," *Transportation Quarterly*, Vol. 49, 1995, pp. 91-104.

189 K. Sale, *Human Scale*, Coward, McCann & Geoghegan, New York, 1980, p. 256.

190 D. Brand, "Research Needs for Analyzing the Impacts of Transportation Options on Urban Form and the Environment," in *Transportation, Urban Form, and the Environment*, Special Report 231, Transportation Research Board, Washington, D.C., 1991, pp. 101-116; A. Downs, *The Need For a New Vision for the Development of Large U.S. Metropolitan Areas*, Salomon Brothers, Bond Market Research, New York, 1989; J. Woodhull, "How Alternative Forms of Development Can Reduce Traffic Congestion," in B. Walter, L. Arkin, and R. Crenshaw (eds.), *Sustainable Cities: Concepts and Strategies for Eco-City Development*, EHM, Los Angeles, 1992, pp. 168-177; T. Beatley, "Planning and Sustainability: The Elements of a New (Improved?) Paradigm," *Journal of Planning Literature*, Vol. 9, 1995, pp. 383-395; R. Cervero, "Paradigm Shift: From Automobility to Accessibility Planning," keynote speech and paper prepared for the 15th EAROPH World Planning Congress, Auckland, New Zealand, September 1996; and Surface Transportation Policy Project (STPP), *A Blueprint for ISTEA Reauthorization: A Common Sense Guide to Transportation Priorities for the 21st Century*, Washington, D.C., 1997, pp. 14-15.

191 This broad definition is misleading: "The concept of *level of service* is defined as a qualitative measure describing operational conditions within a traffic stream, and their perception by motorists and/or passengers. A level-of-service definition generally describes these conditions in terms of such factors as speed and travel time, freedom to maneuver, traffic interruptions, comfort and convenience, and safety." Transportation Research Board (TRB), *Highway Capacity Manual*, Special Report 209, Washington, D.C., 1994, p. 1-3.

192 Transportation Research Board (TRB), op. cit., Table 11-1.

193 Transportation Research Board (TRB), op. cit., Tables 3-1, 7-1, and 8-1.

194 Alan Voorhees & Associates, *Factors and Trends in Trip Lengths*, National Cooperative Highway Research Report 48, Transportation Research Board, Washington, D.C., 1968, pp. 7-10; S.J. Bellomo, R.B. Dial, and A.M. Voorhees, *Factors, Trends, and Guidelines Related to Trip Length*, National Cooperative Highway Research Report 89, Transportation Research Board, Washington, D.C., 1970, pp. 22-31; and K. Neels et al. *An Empirical Investigation of the Effects of Land Use on Urban Travel*, The Urban Institute, Washington, D.C., 1977, pp. 56-60.

195 R. Ewing, "Transportation Service Standards: As If People Matter," *Transportation Research Record 1400*, 1993b, pp. 10-17.

196 Subsections 163.3180(5)(a)-(c); and Rule 9J-5.0055(6), Florida Administrative Code.

197 Subsection 163.3180(7), Florida Statutes; and Rule 9J-5.0055(5), Florida Adminstrative Code.

198 G. Hawthorn, "Transportation Provisions in the Clean Air Act Amendments of 1990," *ITE Journal*, Vol. 61, April 1991, pp. 17-24; Federal Highway Administration (FHWA), *A Summary: Transportation Programs and Provisions of the Clean Air Act Amendments of 1990*, Washingbon, D.C., 1992; G. Hawthorne and M.D. Meyer, *Action Guide for the 1990 Clean Air Act Transportation Provisions*, American Association of State Highway and Transportation Officials (AASHTO), Washington, D.C., 1992; U.S. Environmental Protection Agency (EPA), *1992 Transportation & Air Quality Planning Guidelines*, Office of Mobile Sources, Ann Arbor, Mich., 1992, pp. 15-20, 33-37; and U.S. Environmental Protection Agency (EPA), *VMT Forecasting and Tracking Guidance*, Office of Mobile Sources, Ann Arbor, Mich., 1992.

199 Federal Highway Administration (FHWA), "Management and Monitoring Systems; Interim Final Rule," *Federal Register*, Vol. 58, December 1, 1993, p. 63464.

200 The following language has been interpreted as calling for multimodal performance measures: "Parameters shall...permit the evaluation of the effectiveness of congestion reduction and mobility enhancement strategies for the *movement of people* and goods [emphasis added]." Section 500.507, 23 Code of Federal Regulations.

201 Florida Department of Transportation (FDOT), "How to Measure Mobility," *Florida's Mobility Management Process Work Plan*, Draft of July 5, 1994, pp. 30-45; and D.S. McLeod, "Special Features of Florida's Mobility Management Process," *Transportation Research Record 1552*, 1996, pp. 42-47.

202 Ewing, op. cit., 1993b; R. Ewing, *Roadway Level-of-Service Determination*, Florida Institute of Government, Florida State University, Tallahassee 1991; R. Ewing, "Roadway Levels of Service in an Era of Growth Management," *Transportation Research Record 1364*, 1992, pp. 63-70; Texas Transportation Institute (TTI), *Quantifying Congestion: Interim Report*, National Cooperative Highway Research Program, Transportation Research Board, Washington, D.C., 1992; Center for Urban Transportation Research (CUTR), *The Role of Level of Service Standards in Florida's Growth Management Goals*, University of South Florida, Tampa, 1993; JHK & Associates, *Issues, Options, and Examples: Level of Service Standards/Concurrency Management Systems: Final Report*, Puget Sound Regional Council, Seattle, 1993c; JHK & Associates, *Multi-Modal Transportation Level of Service Policy and Mode-Split Forecasting Tool: Final Report*, Thurston Regional Planning Council, Olympia, Wash., 1993, pp. 1-21 through 1-27; M.F. Reed et al., *Measuring State Transportation Program Performance*, National Cooperative Highway Research Program Report 357, Transportation Research Board, Washington, D.C., 1993; J.P. Savage, E.R. Stollof, and C.W. Wolf, "A Survey of Transportation Service Level Standards," *ITE Journal*, Vol. 63, June 1993, pp. 21-25; Cambridge Systematics, "Task B: Initial Performance Measures," in *Metropolitan Planning Technical Report*, Report No. 2, Federal Highway Administration, Washington, D.C., 1994b; L.D. Frank and C.J. Stone, "Applying GMA Concurrency Requirements to State Highways and Ferries," Office of Urban Mobility, Washington State Department of Transportation, Seattle, 1994; JHK & Associates, "Key Element 3: CMS Performance Measures," *Congestion Management for Technical Staff: Three Day Training Course*, Federal Highway Administration, Washington, D.C., 1994; R.H. Pratt and T.J. Lomax, "Performance Measures for Multimodal Transportation Systems," *Transportation Research Record 1518*, 1996, pp. 85-93; Texas Transportation Institute (TTI), *Methods to Quantify Congestion*, National Cooperative Highway Research Program, Transportation Research Board, Washington, D.C., 1994; D. Samdahl, "Innovative Applications of Level of Service Standards," in J.M. Faris (ed.), *Proceedings of the Fifth Conference on Transportation Planning Methods—Volume I*, Transportation Research Board, Washington, D.C., 1995, pp. 8-27 through 8-33; and S.A. Shbaklo and G.L. Reed, "Measures of Performance for Highway and Transit Systems," *ITE 1996 Compendium of Technical Papers*, Institute of Transportation Engineers, Washington, D.C., 1996, pp. 143-147. Also noteworthy are two ongoing efforts to devise transit performance measures that will become as widely accepted as highway level-of-service measures. One is at the Center for Urban Transportation Research (CUTR) in Tampa, Florida, and the other at the Local Government Commission in Sacramento, California.

203 The following discussion draws principally on four sources: Cambridge Systematics, op. cit, 1994b; Ewing, op. cit., 1993b; JHK & Associates, op. cit.; and Texas Transportation Institute (TTI), op. cit., 1994.

204 M.R. Birdsall, "Vehicle-Miles-of-Travel: Its Use as a Primary Measurement Tool for Traffic Impact Mitigation and Growth Management," unpublished paper available from author, Michael R. Birdsall & Associates, Issaquah, Wash., 1993.

205 California Air Resources Board, *Transportation Performance Standards of the California Clean Air Act*, Sacramento, 1991, pp. 2-3; and Oregon Land Conservation and Development Commission, *Transportation Planning Rule*, Oregon Administration Rule 660-12, Salem, 1991, Section 035(4).

206 State-of-the-practice in regional travel modeling relies on a structure developed decades ago, and largely unchanged for the past 15 years. Models were adequate for the purpose originally intended—the sizing of capital facilities (especially highways). But they fall short of what is required by the Clean Air Act, ISTEA, and Florida's 1993 growth management act. For a critique of conventional models (given new demands), see G. Harvey and E. Deakin, *A Manual of Regional Transportation Modeling Practice for Air Quality Analysis*, National Association of Regional Councils, Washington, D.C., 1993, pp. 3-1 through 3-7.

207 The Florida Department of Transportation has several ongoing projects aimed at enhancing and modernizing the Florida Standard Urban Transportation Model Structure. For national initiatives, see Cambridge Systematics, Inc., *Short-Term Model Improvements*, Technology Sharing Program, U.S. Department of Transportation, Washington, D.C., 1994; G.A. Shunk and P.L. Bass (eds.), *Travel Model Improvement Program: Conference Proceedings*, Technology Sharing Program, U.S. Department of Transportation, Washington, D.C., 1994; E. Weiner and F. Ducca, "Upgrading Travel Demand Forecasting Capabilities," *TR News*, Number 186, September-October 1996, pp. 3-6 and 39; and other publications and newsletter issues of the Travel Model Improvement Program, U.S. Department of Transportation.

208 Ewing, op. cit., 1992; Ewing, op. cit., 1993b; Frank and Stone, op. cit.; and Savage et al., op. cit.

209 Department of City Planning/Department of Public Works, *North San Jose Area Development Policy*, City of San Jose, 1988, pp. 4-7; Orange County Planning Department, *Comprehensive Policy Plan 1990-2010: Traffic Circulation Element*, Orlando, Fla., 1992, pp. 163-166; Planning and Transportation Commission, "Recommended Transportation Policy Framework," City of Bellevue, Wash., 1992; Pierce County Public Works Department, *Service Standards for Arterial Roads*, Pierce County, Wash., 1993, pp. 4-6; King County Parks, Planning and Resources Department, *King County Comprehensive Plan*, Seattle, 1994, pp. 110-112; and Montgomery County Planning Board, *Recommendations for Amending the Methodology for Determining the Adequacy of Transportation Facilities*, Silver Spring, Md., 1994. Also see A.S. Brick-Turin, "Areawide Capacity Analysis," *ITE 1993 Compendium of Technical Papers*, Institute of Transportation Engineers, Washington, D.C., 1993, pp. 473-477.

210 Planning Department, *Transportation Corridors: Meeting the Challenge of Growth Management in Miami*, City of Miami, 1989.

211 Texas Transportation Institute (TTI), op. cit., 1992, p. 55.

212 Ewing, op. cit., 1991; Frank and Stone, op. cit.; Savage et al., op. cit.; ITE Technical Council Committee 6Y-36, "Transportation Elements of Environmental Impact Assessments and Reports," *ITE Journal*, Vol. 58, 1988, pp. 69-75; G. Walters and J.B. Peers, "The Service Level Ordinance as a Growth Management Tool," *ITE 1988 Compendium of Technical Papers*, Institute of Transportation Engineers, Washington, D.C., 1988, pp. 6-11; R.G. Dowling, "Controlling Growth with Level-of-Service Policies," *Transportation Research Record 1237*, 1989, pp. 39-45; W.E. Baumgaertner and J.W. Guckert, "The Evolution of Adequate Public Facilities Ordinances and Their Effectiveness as Growth Management Tools in Maryland," *ITE 1991 Compendium of Technical Papers*, Institute of Transportation Engineers, Washington, D.C., 1991, pp. 52-58; and U. Avin and V. Lazdins, "Understanding Adequate Public Facilities Ordinances," *Land Development*, Vol. 6, Spring-Summer 1993, pp. 25-29.

213 The relationship of accessibility to trip length and VHT is documented in Ewing, op. cit., 1995. Also see Cervero and Kockelman, op. cit.; Handy, op. cit., 1993; S. Hanson, op. cit.; Hanson and Schwab, op. cit.; Parsons Brinckerhoff Quade Douglas, op. cit.; and Williams, op. cit., 1988.

214 Accessibility indices may take many forms, as discussed most recently in Handy, op. cit., 1993; Kitamura et al., op. cit.; Purvis et al., op. cit.; W.B. Allen, D. Liu, and S. Singer, "Accessibility Measures of U.S. Metropolitan Areas," *Transportation Research B*, Vol. 27B, 1993, pp. 439-449; and J. Pooler, "The Use of Spatial Separation in the Measurement of Transportation Accessibility," *Transportation Research A*, Vol. 29A, 1995, pp. 421-427. Standard "four-step" regional travel models such as the Florida Standard Urban Transportation Model Structure (FSUTMS) derive accessibility indices for each zone of origin, and then use them to distribute trips via a gravity model. The higher the index, the more accessible are trip attractions collectively to a given zone.